T
CUSTODY OFFICER'S
COMPANION

by
PAUL HARPER BA
and
STEWART CALLIGAN LLB

First Edition 1993
Second Edition 1995

Also by Stewart Calligan
Points to Prove
Taking Statements

© Paul Harper & Stewart Calligan 1995
ISBN 0 85164 069 9

**POLICE REVIEW
PUBLISHING CO LTD
South Quay Plaza 2
183 Marsh Wall
London E14 9FZ**

Cover Photo by Duncan Ridgley
Illustrations by Rich King
Printed by Cromwell Press, Melksham, Wiltshire

INTRODUCTION

The custody officer is one of the most difficult roles in today's police service.

The custody officer is a creature of statute, conceived in the Royal Commission on Criminal Procedure of 1981 and born in section 66 of the Police and Criminal Evidence Act 1984. He took his first breath in the Codes of Practice which came into force on January 1, 1986 and has been revised by the Criminal Justice and Public Order Act 1994 and the current Codes which commenced on April 10, 1995.

His aim in life is to protect the rights of the individual and the police in the discharge of their duties in this difficult area of the the law.

The Custody Officer's Companion has been designed to unravel the complexities of the job in an easy to read layout. It uses charts, diagrams and illustrations for speed reference. Checklists have been included at key stages of the book for the custody officer's use.

When choosing a custody officer, the prudent manager, in addition to the normal job description, should look for the following attributes, which if not present should be developed:

Fairness

Communication skills

Rapport

Empathy for the arresting officer and the detainee

Interest in the job

Knowledge

Courageousness

Decisiveness

Assertiveness

Adaptability

Paul Harper has recently served as a custody officer, having experience in most areas of police work. He has taught the Police and Criminal Evidence Act 1984 with special emphasis on the job of custody officer. Paul has experienced the old and new approaches to police training.

Stewart Calligan has accepted charges as sergeant and inspector. He has served at the Home Office Central Planning and Training Unit and West Yorkshire Police Training School. Latterly he was in charge of the Humberside Police Training School.

A final word before turning to the book proper. It must be remembered that the general ethos of the Police and Criminal Evidence Act 1984 should be followed — the principles of necessity and accountability.

Regretfully the 1990s will be remembered for the overturning of several high-profile cases. The police cannot be exempt from criticism in these miscarriages of justice.
This illustrates the crucial nature of the principles enacted for the protection of us all.

Keith Hellawell QPM, LLB, MSc
Chief Constable
West Yorkshire Police

CONTENTS

CONTENTS

CONTENTS

CONTENTS

Six   DISPOSAL & CHARGING   177

CONTENTS

Seven SPECIAL GROUPS   209

Eight   SPECIAL PROCEDURES   249

Index   277

CONTENTS

Chapter 1
DETENTION

Detention revolves around the custody officer and the Codes of Practice.

Q What is a custody officer?
A As mentioned in the introduction, under section 36 of the Police and Criminal Evidence Act 1984 the custody officer must be correctly appointed by a chief officer. Note that under section 36(4) an officer of any rank may act as a custody officer if the custody officer is not readily available. What 'readily available' means has not yet been tested in the courts. In the absence of any judicial definition it is felt that reasonableness must prevail.

PACE
S 36

Any officer who accepts a detainee in the absence of a custody officer is acting in the capacity of a custody officer and is then responsible as such.

When the appointed custody officer returns it would be wise to check on the actions of the 'stand in' custody officer and endorse the custody record accordingly. Section 34(2) of the Police and Criminal Evidence Act 1984 stipulates that the custody officer should be satisfied that continued detention is justified.

PACE
S 34

Q What are the Codes of Practice?
A Codes issued by the Home Secretary under PACE which cover (A) Stop and search, (B) Searching of premises, (C) Detention, Treatment and questioning, (D) Identification and (E) Tape recording of interviews.

Q Do the Codes of Practice apply to every one in police custody?
A Generally yes, with certain exceptions

Code C applies to:

- persons under arrest for an offence or otherwise

C
CODE
1.10 & 1.11

- person taken to a place of safety under the Mental Health Act sections 135 and 136

- those arrested under the Prevention of Terrorism (Temporary Provisions) Act 1989.

Code C does not apply to:

- persons arrested by officers from a Scottish force under cross-border powers of arrest

C
CODE
1.12

- people arrested for fingerprinting under the asylum and immigration law

- person served with notice of detention under the Immigration Act 1971

- convicted or remand prisoners held in police cells on behalf of the prison service.

Everyone in police custody comes within Codes 8 and 9 which set out the minimum standards for condition and treatment.

The majority of this book deals with Code C but there are sections of the others which are of importance to custody officer and as such have been included.

All persons in custody must be dealt with as soon as possible and released as soon as the need for detention ends.

C
CODE
1.1, 1.1A
and Note 1H

Although justifiable delays are possible, eg arrest of coach full of football supporters or problems contacting solicitors/interpeters etc, they should be fully documented.

As with most incidents dealt with by the police the medical condition of the detainee is the first consideration.

FIT FOR DETENTION

Q *Is the detainee fit to detain?*
A The custody officer's first
responsibility is to satisfy
himself that there are no
visible or other injuries.

Injuries

He should ask the detainee,
'Are you injured?'
If there are injuries he should
ask,

*'How did you get those
injuries?'*

Good practice dictates that each injury should be recorded
separately on the custody record and alongside each injury the
detainee's explanation of how the injury occurred.

For example:

INJURIES	EXPLANATION
• Bruising to left wrist	Caused by handcuffs
• Cut to left eyebrow scabbed over	Old injury from previous fight
• Graze to knuckles of left hand	Caught on a wall during arrest

This is in effect a negative statement to prevent or discredit any future false allegations of assault.

The detainee should be asked to sign the list of injuries.

Complaints

If the detainee alleges the arresting officer caused the injuries the initial action, such as seizing the officer's clothing, photographs, forensic examinations etc, should immediately be considered.

| C |
| CODE |
| 9.1 |

If a complaint is made by or on behalf of a detained person about his treatment, or any officer discovers that he may have been treated improperly, a report must be made as soon as practicable to an inspector or above who is not connected with the investigation. If the matter concerns an assault or the unnecessary or unreasonable use of force then the police surgeon must also be called.

Where a detainee alleges injury during the course of the arrest but does not wish to make a complaint against the police, this should be recorded and signed by the detainee. Even so, the custody officer may consider it necessary to inform an inspector.

See Code C 9.1 above for circumstances where the custody officer considers that the detainee has been treated improperly, he must report the matter to an Inspector.

Illness

Other useful questions include:

'*Are you taking any medication?*'

'*Are you seeing a doctor for anything?*

'*Have you any medical condition which would put yourself or the police officers at risk?*'

'*Have you taken any alcohol or drugs in the last 24 hours?*'

'*Are you a drug user?*'

The recent events in society put the questions of death in custody, AIDS and Hepatitis B at the forefront of the custody officer's mind.

When in doubt consult a police surgeon, especially when alcohol or drugs are present and more so with any head injury, however minor. A common cause of death whilst drunk is asphyxiation by inhaling vomit.

5

Suicide is also a possibility and custody officers should be constantly on their guard for warning signs, such as previous history, the social stigma associated with the suspected crime and the detainee's own comments and demeanour.

See Chapter 3 for in depth advice in this area.

Information

All sources of information recording the history of the detainee could well be examined at this stage. The custody officer will be looking for a history of violence when in custody, assaulting police officers, a malicious complainer, suicidal, having a contagious disease, escapee and other like matters.

First aid

First aid should always be considered for minor injuries, to protect the police and detainee alike. A recently appointed custody officer should ensure that both he and his staff have had the necessary immunisation against Hepatitis B etc.

Throughout the whole of the first stage of investigating the detainee's medical condition, fully record on the custody record all the information, actions and advice recommended by medical sources. The demeanour of the detainee at this early stage could prove to be relevant and should be recorded when thought necessary, eg the detainee was very co-operative and only too willing to assist, or he was unco-operative, aggressive and abrasive in his manner.

See Chapter 3 for full custody records for medical condition.

SPECIAL GROUPS

Q Which category does the detainee belong to?
A   Mental problems, juvenile, foreigner, blind, deaf, unable to speak, terrorist, Service personnel deserting etc and a drink/ driving suspect or other category.

In the vast majority of cases the detainee will belong to the 'other' category, ie does not fall into one of the special groups which will be dealt with later in the book as follows:

CHECK LIST FOR DETAINEE'S MEDICAL CONDITION

Key questions: *Is he fit to detain?*
Is there any injury, visible or otherwise?

Ascertain from the detainee:

- Any injuries?
- Any medical condition at all?
- Is medication being taken including long-term medication?
- Is there withdrawal from drugs or other drug history?
- Has he any communicable disease?
- Has he had any alcohol?

Which of the following options is the most appropriate?

- Is immediate hospital treatment needed?
  See Chapter 2 for removal to hospital, Code C 9.2

- Does he need examining by a police surgeon or doctor?

- Do you need to consult with a police surgeon?

- Is first aid necessary?

- Does he need special handling, eg protection for officers, isolation or more than normal supervision?

- No medical problem apparent.

OPENING THE CUSTODY RECORD

Q Do I need to open a custody record?
A A custody record must be opened promptly for each person who is brought to a police station under arrest or is arrested at the police station.

All information which has to be recorded under this Code must be recorded as soon as practicable in the custody record unless otherwise specified. Any audio or video recording made in the custody area is not part of the custody record.

VOLUNTARY ATTENDANCE AT POLICE STATION

Section 29 Police and Criminal Evidence Act 1984 deals with voluntary attendance at police stations, viz:

PACE
S 29

Where a person attends voluntarily at a police station to assist the police with their enquiries or accompanies a constable to a police station without having been arrested:

C
CODE
3.15 & 3.16

- He is entitled to leave at will.
- He shall be told at once that he is under arrest if a constable decides to prevent him from leaving.

Therefore, if the suspect had attended the police station voluntarily and was being interviewed by a constable, then if the constable decides to arrest him, he should be taken before the custody officer and the rest of Code C should be put into practice.

If the person is cautioned but not arrested the constable must tell him he is not under arrest, is free to leave at will, and should administer the legal formula as follows.

Legal advice formula

The person concerned must be told he is

- entitled to FREE and INDEPENDENT legal advice
- entitled to speak to a solicitor on the telephone and asked if he wishes to do so and if he asks about legal advice be provided with a legal advice notice.

ARREST ELSEWHERE THAN AT THE POLICE STATION

**PACE
S 30**

Section 30 Police and Criminal Evidence Act 1984 deals with the arrest elsewhere than at a police station, viz:

- When a person is arrested by a constable for an offence, or is accepted into custody after being arrested for an offence by some other person at some other place, eg store detective

- he shall be taken to a police station by a constable as soon as practicable after the arrest.

DESIGNATED POLICE STATION

The police station should be a designated police station. *See note 2 for exceptions.*

PACE
S 30(2)

NOTE ONE

It has been said that certain police officers have been delaying the taking of a detainee to a designated police station after arrest. The reason for such action is said to be to allow the arresting officer to interview the detainee in the back of the police car avoiding the rigours of the Police and Criminal Evidence Act. It may well be impossible to stop a suspect admitting offences on the way to a police station but such admissions will be given close attention in court.

NOTE TWO

There are occasions when the detainee may be taken to a police station which is not designated under this Act, ie

PACE
S 30(3-5)

Where it appears that the detainee will not be in custody for more than six hours and the officer concerned is:

- a constable who is working in a locality covered by a police station which is not a designated police station; and

- a constable belonging to a body of constables maintained by an authority other than a police authority;

or

Where the arrest was by a constable or by another person but without assistance of any constable and no other constable is available to assist;

and

It appears to the constable that he cannot take him to a designated station without the detainee injuring himself, the constable or some other person.

Transfer to a designated police station

PACE
S 30(6)

If the first police station to which an arrested person is taken is not designated, he shall be taken to a designated police station within six hours after his arrival at the first police station unless he is released previously.

NOTE ONE

Transfers of this kind occur where persons are arrested at or taken to small non-designated stations or to temporary stations at football grounds, events etc before being transferred to designated stations with full facilities. Obviously the custody record will reflect this transfer.

NOTE TWO

Delays also occur when detainees are injured on or prior to arrest and are taken elsewhere for medical treatment before arriving at a police station.

RELEASE FROM ARREST

PACE
S 30(7-9)

A person arrested by a constable shall be released if a constable is satisfied, before the person arrested arrives at a police station, that there are no grounds for keeping him under arrest. He does not have to be brought into the custody suite or entered onto a custody record. The constable should simply record what he has done.

The constable shall make the record as soon as is practicable after the release.

DELAY IN TAKING A PERSON TO A POLICE STATION

There is nothing to prevent an officer delaying taking a person under arrest to a police station if the the person is required elsewhere in order to pursue immediate reasonable inquiries, eg to recover abandoned stolen property.

PACE
S 30(10)

NOTE ONE

Where there is such a delay the reasons for it shall be recorded when the person arrives at a police station.

PACE
S 30(11)

NOTE TWO

Subsection (11) places a duty on the custody officer to enquire when he was arrested and then compare the time of arrival at the police station. Any discrepancies will then be documented together with the reasons for the delay.

Exceptions

PACE
S 30(12-13)

There are certain exceptions to section 30(1) PACE:

- Paragraphs 16(3) and 18(1) of Schedule 2 to the Immigration Act 1971;

- Section 34(1) of the Criminal Justice Act 1972; and

- Paragraph 5 of Schedule 3 to the Prevention of Terrorism (Temporary Provisions) Act 1984 or any provision contained in an order under section 13 of that Act which authorises the detention of persons on board a ship or aircraft.

Another exception is found in section 30(10). Nothing in that subsection shall be taken to affect paragraph 18(3) of Schedule 2 to the Immigration Act 1971.

The arresting officer will, in many cases look to the custody officer for help and advice. The custody officer should be ready to help in such cases as all arresting officers will differ in levels of experience. It could be their first or their one hundredth arrest.

DRUGS SEARCHES

NOTE

That under the Misuse of Drugs Act 1971 section 23(2) a constable may 'detain' a person for the purpose of searching him. It could be argued that a 'detention' under drugs law for the purpose of searching is not an arrest. However if the detainee is brought to the police station then it is suggested that the custody officer should deal with the matter as if he were detained under the provisions of PACE and record the events on a custody record. The rights normally accorded to an arrested person would not apply.

CHILDREN ACT

NOTE

When children are in police protection as outlined in the Children Act 1989 they should not be detained in the custody suite and a custody record should not be kept.

COMPLETING THE CUSTODY RECORD

Q How do I complete these forms?
A Read back through old custody records to familiarise yourself with the problems your custody officer colleagues have had. Use an indelible roller ball pen or felt-tip pen as opposed to something that could be erased.

Some forces use computerised records and typewritten records. Where writing is the norm the custody officer must write clearly and legibly. The making of the custody record is often done under conditions of bad language, telephones ringing, bad light, incorrectly angled desks or wrong height of tables etc. It is up to the custody officer to make his working environment as comfortable as possible.

The custody record requires:

- Legibility
- Brevity
- Accuracy

It must be remembered that the custody record may be closely scrutinised by:

- Other custody officers
- Review officers
- Superintendent
- Prosecution staff
- Crown Prosecution Service
- Solicitors and barristers
- Courts
- Discipline and complaints officers

The proficient completion of custody records will also reflect on the custody officer's competence and will sometimes be the only paperwork his supervisors will have access to, on which to base the appraisal of his performance.

A Specimen Custody Record

Police Station   **Code**   **Other refs:**   **Custody number**

1. Reason for arrest . . . .
    . . . .

2. Arrested persons comments. . . . .
    . . . .

NB Custody officer should NOTE but not invite comments when
    arresting officer gives reasons for arrest.
    For signature statements see Code C11.13
    C/Officers' signature. . . . .
    Detention time . . . .   Date. . . . .

3.

	Time	Date
Arrested		
Arrived at Station		
Relevant time		

4. Place of arrest . . . .
    . . . .

5. Detention Decision
    Authorised/Not Authorised*
    Signature . . . . Name . . . .
    Time . . . . Date . . . .

    Reason for Detention

(i) To charge. . . . . ☐   Record grounds for detention .
&/or (ii) other. . . . . ☐   . . . .
&/or (iii) To secure or preserve   Person present when grounds
evidence. . . . . ☐   recorded   YES ☐ NO ☐
&/or (iv) To detain evidence   Person informed of grounds
by questioning. . . . . ☐   YES ☐ NO ☐

6. Comment re detention decision . . . .
    . . . .
    Custody Officers Signature . . . .
    Time . . . . Date . . . .

7. Personal Details
    Surname . . . . Forename(s). . . . .
    Former Surname . . . .

*Delete as appropriate   Cont

Continued from previous page

Address. . . . .
. . . .
Occupation . . . .
Age . . . .   Date of birth . . . .
Height . . . .   Sex Male/Female . . . .
Ethnic origin . . . .   Place of birth . . . .

8. Arresting Officer . . . .
Rank . . . . . .   No. . . . .   Stn/Branch . . . .

9. Officer in case . . . .
Rank . . . . . .   No. . . . .   Stn/Branch . . . .

10. Detained Person's Rights
An extract from a notice setting out my rights has been read to
me and I have been given a copy. I have also been provided
with a written notice setting out my entitlements while in custody.
     Signature . . . .
     Time . . . .   Date . . . .
I want a solicitor as soon as practicable:
     Signature . . . .
I do not want a solicitor at this time:
     Signature . . . .
Reasons given . . . .
I do not wish to speak to a duty solicitor on the telephone
and I hereby confirm that I do not want a solicitor at this time.
     Signature . . . .
     Time . . . .   Date . . . .
I have spoken to a duty solicitor on the telephone and I now
WANT/DON'T WANT a solicitor.
     Signature . . . .   Time . . . .   Date . . . .
Noti cation of named person requested   YES ☐ NO ☐
Details of nominated person . . . .

11. Appropriate Adult/Interpreter
Notices served, rights and grounds for detention explained in
presence of appropriate adult/Interpreter
Signature of appropriate adult/Interpreter . . . .
Time . . . .   Date . . . .

12. Foreign Nationals
Embassy/Consulate informed   YES ☐

Authority

When authority is given for any action under PACE by an officer of any rank, his name and rank must be noted in the custody record.

C CODE 2.2

NOTE

This does not apply to officers dealing with persons detained under the Prevention of Terrorism (Temporary Provisions) Act 1989, in which case the record is limited to the warrant or other identification number and duty station.

Accuracy

The custody officer is responsible for making a full and accurate custody record.

C CODE 2.3

Copies

Transfers: The custody officer is responsible for ensuring that either the record or a copy accompanies a detainee transferred to another police station.

C CODE 2.3

NOTE ONE

The record shall show the time & reason for the transfer and the time of a detainee's release.

When a person leaves police detention or is taken before a court, the following shall be supplied on request with a copy record as soon as practicable: the detainee, his legal representative or his appropriate adult.

C CODE 2.4

NOTE TWO
This entitlement lasts 12 months

When such a record is given the custody officer would be wise to ensure that
- a copy is attached to the crime file or
- a copy is sent to CPS when the file has already been sent.

Inspection

A solicitor or appropriate adult should be allowed to inspect the custody record as soon as practicable after they arrive at the police station.

C C CODE 2.4

| C CODE 2.5 |

When a person leaves police detention – the appropriate adult, or the legal representative who gives reasonable notice of a request, may inspect the custody record.

A note of the inspection must be made on the record.

| C CODE 2.6 |

Timing

All entries must be timed and signed by the maker.

NOTE

Special provisions exist in relation to computer records and for persons detained under the Prevention of Terrorism (Temporary Provisions) Act 1989.

Refusal

| C CODE 2.7 |

When a person refuses to sign the record this itself must be recorded.

LAWFUL ARREST

Q Has the person before you been lawfully arrested?

A The choice includes:

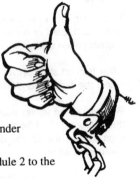

- For an arrestable offence, section 24 Police and Criminal Evidence Act 1984.

- The general arrest conditions under section 25 of the above Act.

- The preserved powers in Schedule 2 to the above Act.

- Warrant

- Common Law. Note that the common law power of arrest revolves around the Queen's Peace. (See post)

NOTE

Cross-border enforcement

Criminal Justice and Public Order Act 1994 Sections 136-140 These sections extend the jurisdiction of police officers across borders, ie to arrest without a warrant, or execute warrants in all parts of the United Kingdom. Thus custody officers will be presented with prisoners arrested in

Scotland or Northern Ireland by officers from their own force, or have to accept persons arrested by officers from Northern Ireland or Scottish forces.

Warrants

A warrant to arrest an offender may be issued when information is laid before a magistrate to the effect that the suspect has or is suspected of having committed an offence.

The execution of an arrest warrant is valid until the warrant is withdrawn and can be executed anywhere in the United Kingdom.

The Magistrates' Courts Act 1980 section 97 provides that where a magistrate is satisfied that a person who could give material evidence would not voluntarily attend court, then a warrant may be issued.

A warrant to commit to prison is a warrant of arrest directing that the person be taken to a specified place. On arrest the constable should take the person to the place specified and obtain a receipt.

POSSESSION OF WARRANT WHEN EXECUTING

By virtue of section 125 of the Magistrates' Courts Act 1980 (as amended) the following warrants do not need to be in the possession of the constable at the time:

- Warrants to arrest a person in connection with an offence;

- Warrants under the Army Act 1955, Air Force Act 1955, Naval Discipline Act 1957 or Reserve Forces Act 1980 (desertion etc);

- Warrants for insufficiency of distress (under sections 102 or 104 of the General Rate Act 1967);

- Warrants for the protection of a party to a marriage or of a child of the family (under section 18 of the Domestic Proceedings and Magistrates' Courts Act 1978); and

- Warrants relating to the non-appearance of a defendant, warrants of commitment in default of payment of a fine or maintenance, warrants to arrest a witness in criminal proceedings (under sections 55, 76, 93 and 97 of the Magistrates' Courts Act 1980).

But in such cases the warrant must, on the demand of the person concerned, be shown to him as soon as practicable. In *De Costa Small v Kirkpatrick* [1979] Crim LR 41, it was held that a warrant for a civil matter was not in the officer's possession when it was at a police station half a mile away.

When the detainee is arrested on warrant it is strongly advised that the custody officer checks the warrant to ensure that:

- It refers to the prisoner;
- He takes the required action for that type of warrant;
- It is current;
- Should any money be paid?
- Is the warrant backed for bail?

If it is, the custody officer would then bail to the appropriate court. NB Special courts exist for certain matters ie fines. Care should be taken to bail to the right court on the right day.

The arresting officer should endorse the warrant after execution.

CUSTODY RECORD – WARRANTS

Brief details of the warrant should be shown on the custody record eg:

- Arrest warrant for non-payment of £1,000 fine issued on 1.4.95 by Some town Magistrates.

- Not backed for bail

- Reference number 624/95

- A photostate copy of the warrant could also be attached to the custody record and clearly marked (COPY)

- Explanation from arresting officer

Breach of the Peace

The Queen's Peace or the 'Public Peace' is a difficult term to define but is generally understood as relating to the normal and ordered state of society. Any unlawful disturbance of this normal state will usually constitute a 'breach of the peace'.

North v Pullen [1962] Crim LR 97, provides authority for a constable to arrest any person who in his presence commits a breach of the peace if the arrest is effected at the time when, or immediately after, the offence is committed or while there is danger of its renewal.

A probelm associated with a breach of the peace is the necessity to produce witnesses, including police officers, before the 'next available court'. An alternative would be to consider substantive offences allowing bail to a convenient court date.

ACCEPTING THE ARREST

Q How should the arresting officer explain to the custody officer the reason for the arrest?

A Normally the arresting officer will state the offence and outline the circumstances surrounding the arrest.

This should be done in the prisoner's sight and hearing as

C
CODE
3.4

23

important challenges can be made at this stage by the detainee. The custody officer should record any comments but should not invite them.

The custody officer should then confirm with the detainee that he understands that he has been arrested and what he has been arrested for.

Examples of reasons for arrest and power of arrest:

- Custody officer informed by PC 1234 Bainbridge:

    Information has been received that the prisoner has handled 24 bottles of malt whisky which had been stolen from Dino's Restaurant on 24 March 95.

    I have arrested him for handling stolen goods which is an arrestable offence.

- Custody officer informed by PC 5678 Hellawell:

    I saw the prisoner jump on the bonnet of a Ford Sierra Saloon motor car the property of Mr Dickinson and cause two large dents.

    I have arrested him for criminal damage which is an arrestable offence.

- Custody officer informed by PC57 Smith:

    I was deliberately pushed by the prisoner into a sharp topped fence at the football match.

    I have arrested him for assaulting a police officer, under the Police Act.

- Custody officer informed by PC49 Atidor:

    This man has given a positive breath test after driving a motor vehicle on a road and I have detained him under the Road Traffic Act.

- Custody officer informed by PC 4273 Rose:

  Information has been received that the prisoner dumped two old fridges onto moor land at the side of London Road, Some town.

  I have arrested him under the general arrest condition as he refused to identify himself.

- Custody officer informed by PC69 Terry:

  This youth has taken a motor car without the owner's consent.

  He has been arrested under the Police and Criminal Evidence Act which make this an arrestable offence.

- Custody officer informed by PC 16 Heads:

  I saw the prisoner singing, shouting and urinating in a busy street. His eyes were glazed, he was unsteady on his feet and his breath smelled of intoxicating liquor, beer or lager or the like. I arrested him for being drunk and disorderly.

One of the above has not got a power of arrest. You as a custody officer should spot this and give advice. There is no power of arrest for assaulting a constable but if injury or a breach of the peace were involved or the general arrest conditions section. 25 PACE applied, a power of arrest could be present.

ADVICE FROM CUSTODY OFFICER

In some cases the arresting officer will seek the advice of the custody officer regarding the legal and other aspects of the case. This could well occur before the officer is ready to explain formally the reasons for the arrest and the power of arrest.

For example the officer may ask for advice on a technical legal matter or to explain the confidential nature of the evidence such as evidence from an informant who is known to the detainee.

As far a possible the reasons for such discussions should be explained to the detainee to remove doubt and suspicion from his mind.

CONFIDENTIAL INFORMANTS

In cases where the arrest is based on confidential information or from someone who is known to the suspect, it is suggested that the custody officer simply tells the detainee that he is satisfied that the arrest is lawful, eg the thief who informs on the handler of stolen property. The custody officer would explain that he is satisfied that there is evidence to show that the detainee has handled stolen goods, namely, 24 bottles of malt whisky.

If the custody officer foresees the need to record the more confidential side of the informant's evidence he could use his official note book and cross-reference the entry with the custody record. In this way he could vindicate his actions at some future date without breaching the informant's confidentiality. He would merely show 'from information received' on the custody record.

OFFICER OTHER THAN ARRESTING OFFICER

Where an officer other than the arresting officer brings a detainee to the police station the custody officer should decide whether to accept the arrest from the officer present or wait for the actual arresting officer. If the arresting officer is not going to be unduly late he could wait. Conversely, where a long delay is expected he could accept the explanation for the arrest from the escorting officer. It is advised that in such cases, the circumstances are confirmed with the actual arresting officer as soon as practicable.

NOTIONAL ARRESTS

It is worthy of note that some persons detained are liable to be arrested for further offences which they are not aware of. Section 31 Police and Criminal Evidence Act 1984 states: where

PACE
S 31

- A person is arrested and detained for an offence and

- if he were released, he would be liable to arrest for some other offence, **he shall be arrested for that offence.**

The objective of this section is to ensure the prisoner knows all the reasons for detention to allow him to make informed decisions as to his rights and entitlements.

UNLAWFUL DETENTION

Q How does the custody officer release a person whom he decides has been unlawfully detained?
A The detainee should be released immediately, unconditionally, with an apology and an explanation as to what had happened.

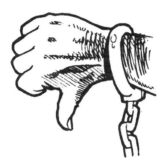

Fairness is paramount and consideration should be given to returning him from where he came.

A custody record should be kept in such cases and endorsed with the action as explained above. The custody officer should seek the cooperation of the detainee for the final completion of the custody record, but care should be taken not to keep him under arrest for this purpose.

NOTE

PACE
S 30(7)

The circumstances covered by section.30(7) PACE 1984 where the arresting officer should release a detainee prior to arriving at a police station when it becomes apparent that there are no grounds for keeping him under arrest.

IS DETENTION NECESSARY

Q Is it necessary to detain this person?
A This is the application of the necessity principle underpinning the Police and Criminal Evidence Act.

The arrest was at the arresting officer's discretion. The detention is now at the custody officer's discretion. Acceptance of detention is the next stage after the custody officer has decided that the detainee has been lawfully arrested.

As well as operating legal criteria, the custody officer exercises wider considerations based on compassion, common sense and cost effectiveness. Hence detention may not be applicable for some old people, some juveniles, some mentally ill persons and offences such as some types of shoplifting and minor damage.

AUTHORISING DETENTION

Section 37 Police and Criminal Evidence Act 1984 provides:

1: Where:

PACE
S 37(1-3)

- A person is arrested for an offence:
  (i) without warrant; or
  (ii) under a no bail warrant or,

- A person answers bail,

the custody officer must decide whether there is evidence to charge him and may detain him long enough to do so.

2: If the custody officer decides there is not sufficient evidence to charge, the person arrested shall be released with or without bail, unless he has reasonable grounds for believing that detention without charge is necessary to secure or preserve evidence relating to an offence for which he has been arrested or to obtain such evidence by questioning him.

NOTE
Subsection (1) deals with the detention of the prisoner until tho custody officer decides that there is sufficient evidence for a charge to be made.

Subsection (2) places a duty on the custody officer to release the prisoner either on bail or without bail when there is insufficient evidence for a charge, unless:

- He has reasonable grounds to believe that detention is necessary;
- To secure or preserve evidence for the offence he has been arrested for; or
- To obtain such evidence by questioning him.

Subsection (3) states that when he has such reasonable grounds he may authorise detention. This is the investigative area of the Act and the officer dealing with the case must now act fast to collect and compile the available evidence.

CUSTODY RECORD

Where a custody officer authorises the detention of a person who has not been charged, **he shall**:

PACE
S 37(4)

- Record the grounds for the detention in the presence of the detainee
- Promptly inform him of the grounds for detention (before he is questioned regarding any offence)
- Record any comments made without inviting such comments.

The custody officer **shall not** question him regarding any of the following:

- his participation in any offence
- his comments on the arresting officer's account
- His comments on the grounds for detention

C
CODE
3.4

as any such questions could be construed as an interview.

29

NOTE

This duty placed on the custody officer is based on the rule of natural justice that a person should know the grounds of his detention and the nature of the allegations.

The above can be postponed where the person arrested is,

PACE
S 37(6)

- Incapable of understanding what is said to him;

- Violent or likely to become violent; or

- In urgent need of medical attention.

This is a much complained of area. It is perhaps the subjective element that must be exercised by the custody officer that causes the problem. Suffice it to say that the prudent custody officer will tread carefully here. If his decision is to delay the making of the custody record etc he should at least make a note of why he made such a decision eg:

- The detainee was drunk, drugged or otherwise incapable of understanding;

- That he was violent at the time or there was every indication that he would become violent; or

- He was loosing blood from a cut left wrist and needed urgent medical attention.

In such cases the custody records and informing him of the grounds of detention should wait. But it should not be forgotten and must be carried out later.

CHARGE OR RELEASE

Subject to section 41(7) (the 24 hour rule), if the custody officer decides that he has enough evidence to charge the person arrested with the offence for which he was arrested, the person:

PACE
S 37(7)

- Shall be charged; or

- Shall be released without charge, with or without bail.

NOTE

Charging will be dealt with in more depth at Chapter 6; section 41(7) deals with how long suspects can be detained.

Where:

- A person is released without charge, with or without bail, and

- At that time a decision whether to prosecute for the offence has not been taken, the custody officer shall so inform him.

PACE
S 37(8)

Unfit to charge or release

If the person arrested is not in a fit state to be charged or released, he may be detained until he is.

PACE
S 37(9)

NOTE

He can be detained until he is in a fit state to be dealt with.

TIMING

The duty imposed under subsection (1), ie to detain until he decides whether to charge, shall be carried out by the custody officer as soon as practicable after the suspect's arrival at the police station or, if arrested at the police station, as soon as practicable after the arrest.

PACE
S 37(10)

NOTE

This subsection lays down a time-scale for the custody officer to act as soon as practicable after the arrest. That is in relation to determining whether there is sufficient evidence on which to charge the prisoner.

THE DETAINED PERSON'S PROPERTY

C CODE 4.1 Code C 4.1 deals with the detained person's property. It lays down what a custody officer is responsible for:

1	Ascertaining	6	Protection
2	Searching	7	Explanation
3	DIY	8	Directions
4	Sex	9	Booby traps
5	Sharp objects		

1 Ascertaining

- The property a detained person has with him when he comes in the police station, whether:

    (i) on arrest,

    (ii) re-detention on answering to bail,

    (iii) commitment to prison custody on the order or sentence of a court,

    (iii) lodgement at the police station with a view to his production in court from such custody,

    (iv) arrival at a police station on transfer from detention at another station or from hospital, or

    (v) on detention under sections 135 or 136 of the Mental Health Act 1983.

- The property he might have acquired for an unlawful or harmful purpose while in custody.

- The safe keeping of property taken from him and kept at the police station.

2 Searching

Q Should I search the detainee or ask someone else to search him or not search him at all?

A The necessity principle again applies.

C
CODE
4.1

PACE explains that not all detainees need be searched, eg where a person will only be detained a short time and will not be placed in a cell.

C
CODE
4.A

In such cases the custody record must be endorsed 'Not searched' and the person invited to sign the entry. If he refuses to sign, the custody officer may be obliged to search him.

3 DIY

Where search is decided upon it has been found useful to ask the detainee to 'turn out or empty his pockets' or 'her handbag etc'. In this way the detainee may wish to conceal something. When the concealed article is found by the subsequent search the fact that the article was concealed could have evidential significance at a later date, eg a burglar keeping a particular key at the bottom of his pocket.

4 Sex

After the detainee has emptied his pockets the custody officer or an officer authorised by him (of the same sex as the detainee) should then make a thorough search.

5   Sharp objects

The procedure can cause conflict and the searching officer should be on guard against being attacked or injured by drug needles or other sharp things.

6   Protection

Officers should take great care given the risk of blood-borne infections such as HI or Hepatitis B.The custody officer should ensure that the searching officer wears protective disposable gloves where possible. In any case the searching officer should not have any broken skin which could allow infection to enter his body. For more information see HOC 113/92.

7   Explanation

Good practice dictates that the custody officer explains fully to the detainee that a search is to be made and the extent of that search; that the gloves are necessary as a general protective measure and that such a search is designed to protect the public and the police.

8   Directions

It will also be wise for the custody officer to direct the search in many cases due to his accumulated knowledge in this area.

9   Booby traps

Be aware of the occasional 'booby trapped' property with contaminated hypodermic needles and other sharp objects placed in such a way as specifically to injure officers.Examples include leaving razor blades in pockets or embedding hypodermic needles into car seats of vehicles about to be recovered or seized by the police.

STRIP SEARCHES AND INTIMATE BODY SEARCHES

Q   What do I need to consider before a strip search and an intimate body search?

C
CODE
4.1 & ANNEX A

A 1 Strip searches

This is a search involving the removal of anything more than outer clothing. This search operates on the necessity principle, ie not carried out as a matter of routine and only as necessity demands.

It must be authorised by the custody officer, only when he reasonably considers that an article might have been concealed which the person would not be allowed to keep.

Annex A(B) sets out a program for strip searches.

- SAME SEX - The officer searching must be of the same sex
- PRIVACY - The person searched must not be seen by anyone except those person(s) necessary for the search and an appropriate adult where necessary.
- TWO PRESENT - Except in urgent cases - there must be at least 2 persons present when:

risk of serious harm

exposure of intimate parts

juvenile, mentally disordered, mentally handicapped, [extra person must be an appropriate adult, though the appropriate adult need not be present if both the juvenile and appropriate adult agree]

- SENSITIVITY - Whenever possible allow the person to remain partly clothed at all times ie replace upper garment before removing lower ones
- VISUAL - Require the person being searched to spread arms and legs and bend to facilitate the examination of genital and anal areas. There must be no physical contact with any orifice which could constitute an intimate or non-intimate search.
- REMOVAL OF ARTICLES - Articles found must be handed over by the prisoner as removal could constitute an intimate search under Annex A(A), the exception being the mouth, ie 'Search upon Arrest'

PACE
S 32(4)
As Amended

- SPEED - The search should be done quickly to allow the person to dress

A 2 Intimate searches

Once again this type of search operates on the principles of necessity and accountability. In practice, common sense and decency are the watchwords of the custody officer.

Body orifices other than the mouth may be searched by a medical practitioner or nurse only where a superintendent or above has reasonable grounds for believing that:

- An article which could cause physical injury is concealed; or
- A Class A drug, intended for supply or export; is concealed and
- An intimate search is the only practicable means of removing it

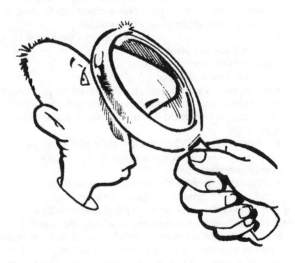

NOTE ONE

This information could be obtained by questioning the detainee eg 'Are you a drugie?' or from the arresting officer, or from PNC or force information systems, or from items in the prisoner's possession etc. This procedure should be fully explained by the custody officer and the prisoner's cooperation sought.

Note the additional records the custody officer must make for intimate and strip searches.

NOTE TWO

Be aware of the restrictions placed on this type of search:

- On the person searching;

- On those allowed to be present; and

- The place where the search can be made.

See Annex A(A) to Code C for full details.

CUSTODY RECORD – SEARCHES

Must

- Record the reason for the search and what type it is
- In strip search of juvenile, record decision of juvenile and appropriate adult,.ie adults presence.
- Record the result of the search
- When not searched endorse record accordingly

Advised to record

- Who authorised and who was present when the search took place

0947   Strip search authorised by custody officer, Sergeant Wetherby for evidential purposes, ie believed stolen money secreted. Custody sergeant and PC Smith (jailer) present, who did the search in the cell.

PERSONAL PROPERTY

C
CODE
4.2

Q *Can the detainee retain his clothing and personal effects?*
A Under Code C 4.2 a detainee may retain property at his own risk unless the custody officer considers:

- That he may use them to cause harm to himself or others;

- That he may use them to interfere with evidence;

- That he may use them to damage property;

- That he may use them to effect an escape; or

- That they are needed as evidence in the event of any of these points applying. The custody officer may withhold such articles as he sees fit. If he does so he must give the reason.

Personal effects

C
CODE
4.3

'Personal effects' are things the person may need while being detained. They do not include cash or valuable items

NOTE
It is thought that 'personal effects' include: handkerchief, comb, spectacles, diary, writing equipment, cigarettes.

Danger areas include matches and lighters and it is recommended that these are retained by the custody officer. Custody staff are advised to carry lighters for the prisoners' needs.

Watches, and items of personal jewellery should be retained by the custody officer but a lenient application of his discretion may be appropriate eg rings and earrings which may be difficult to remove or of extreme sentimental value to the detainee. It seems pointless for officers to put themselves at risk in removing such items for the sake of bureaucracy.

Care should be taken to endorse the custody record clearly showing the collection of items retained by the prisoner eg:

Retained: By Jones: Wedding ring, gold-rimmed spectacles, comb plastic, diary, handkerchief.

Items taken from the detainee will be entered under the appropriate part of the custody record.

PRISONER'S PROPERTY

CASH
- Five x ten £ notes
- Two x fifty pence pieces
  Total   £51.00

HARM
- Shoes
- Penknife

EVIDENCE Glass cutter
(seized as evidence by PC 57
M Nattrass ref OTFP 123)

C CODE 4.5

C CODE 4.4

'Cash, harm, evidence' these reasons are required to be recorded per Code C 4.5.

The prisoner must be asked to sign the list of property and any refusal noted.

NOTE

Where prisoners share cells a more stringent policy of taking possession of items should be applied to prevent property being exchanged, stolen, or lost etc.

It is advised that custody officers meet, and agree on a common policy, determining what they will allow the prisoner to retain. Otherwise prisoners see different rules applied and may become paranoid, eg 'Why me?'

However there are always exceptions and it is not worth exposing an officer or a prisoner to harm, just to prove a point! Common sense must prevail.

Variations

Variations in a prisoner's property can occur when items are purchased, transferred or received, subsequent to the initial record being made.

Purchase
This occurs when the custody officer allows the prisoner to buy items such as cigarettes, toiletries etc.

Transferred property
Occurs when the custody officer allows property to be given to a relative or friend at the prisoner's request.

Received
Relatives and friends are prone to bring clothing, food and money etc for the use of the detainee.

NOTE

In all these cases the custody officer should exercise caution and be aware of the many ulterior motives that may be behind such matters. Records should be constantly up-dated in relation to the property list. The prisoner's signature should always be obtained and that of the persons taking or receiving such property.

- Prisoners' property together with evidence in a case is initially the responsibility of the custody officer. It should not be left unattended or insecure.

- It is also helpful to know what the local prison will accept in relation to property.

Unsuitable property

PACE provides that the custody officer does not need to record, property if due to its nature, quantity or size, it is not practicable to remove it to the police station.

C
CODE
4B

NOTE

This includes all manner of things unsuitable by virtue of:

Size   Vehicles, stores, equipment
Danger   Chemicals, firearms, explosives
Perishable   Flowers, plants, foodstuffs
Requiring special conditions
                   Animals, furs, certain antiques etc

Keeping such articles consumes all manner of police resources and often leads to complaints and aggravation to all concerned.

CLOTHING

PACE does not require that items of clothing be recorded unless kept by the custody officer in accordance with paragraph 4.2. In some circumstances the custody officer may decide a description of the clothing worn by the detainee is worthy of note in the custody record for any future identification purpose. Similarly instant pictures of prisoners can be very useful for later identification (though there is no power to take them).

C
CODE
4C

CUSTODY RECORD – PROPERTY

The custody officer is responsible for recording all property brought to the police station that a detained person had with him, or had taken from him on arrest.

The detained person shall be allowed to check and sign the record of property as correct.

Any refusal to sign should be recorded.

If a detained person is not allowed to keep any article of clothing or personal effects the reason must be recorded.

NOTE

A cautionary note about prisoners' property is that it has been the cause of officers being disciplined, occasionally being dismissed and even imprisoned. The careful recording and secure storage is essential.

TRANSFERS TO AND FROM A POLICE STATION

*Q How does the custody officer deal with a detainee arriving
    from another police station or somewhere else?*

A PACE provides that the right not to be held incommunicado
   applies at each new police station he is taken to. See Chapter
   2.

C
CODE
5.3

The fine detail is usually covered in the force standing orders.

Transfers can be:

- To another police station within force area.

- From another police station within force area.

- To courts.

- To other forces.

- To prisons or remand centres.

Police station – Out

In a nutshell, transfer from a police station to another station in
the same force area is a simple matter. At the releasing station the
custody officer will contact the receiving station to arrange the
transfer. He should check the prisoner's condition, the condition
of the cell he is vacating, the property, and be in a position to
advise the escorting officer and make the necessary entries in the
custody record and on other force forms and books, where
necessary.

Police station – In

The custody officer at the receiving station should examine the
condition of the prisoner and check the property in the presence
of the escorting officer, ie that any seals are intact.

He should open a custody record and inform the prisoner of his
rights to have someone informed of his whereabouts etc, see
Chapter 2. Any 'body receipt' and empty property bag, where
appropriate, should be sent back to the releasing station.

To courts

After being charged the relevant time stops. A custody record should still be maintained. Once in the custody of a court, PACE does not apply, although in practice records are normally maintained.

To other forces

Transfer to other forces is common where a person has been arrested on behalf of that other force. The receiving force normally provides the escort. When the escort arrives the custody officer should examine the condition of the prisoner, the cell he has vacated, the property and make the appropriate records on the custody record.

To prison

Transfers to prison are normally on remand or for a custodial sentence. The custody officer should arrange for a suitable escort. He should carefully examine the property and be aware of certain items that HM Prisons will not accept (such as a watch with a stopwatch mechanism or rings with 'stones').

Any property not sent to prison should be dealt with according to force practice. Remember body receipt procedures and 'Exceptional Risk' forms if appropriate.

The custody record should be completed and any other forms or books dealt with.

Women committed with babies should be discussed with the prison governor immediately it is known. This is to pave the way for the prison authorities to make arrangements for the child. Sometimes prisons have no accommodation for babies and the problem is then back in the custody officer's court. Arrangements with friends, relatives and, as a last resort, social services must then be considered. It is imperative that the existence of the baby and the woman's wishes are made known to the court before it reaches a decision.

WHAT IS AN EXCEPTIONAL RISK PRISONER?

Q What is an exceptional risk prisoner?
A One who:
- Is of an extremely violent nature.
- May have suicidal tendencies.
- May try to bring drugs into custody.
- Is likely to try to escape.
- Associates with dangerous people who may try a rescue.
- May be charged with other serious offences.
- Is physically ill or mentally disturbed.
- Has some other reason.

Exceptional risk prisoners

Q What does the custody officer do with an exceptional risk prisoner?
A When an officer suspects his prisoner falls into an exceptional risk category he should bring that to the custody officer's attention. When the custody officer personally suspects that a prisoner is of exceptional high risk or he has had it brought to his attention, an 'Exceptional Risk Form' should be completed. This form should accompany the detainee to other places of detention to warn the different custodians of the exceptional risk. The prisoner's behaviour should be monitored and the risk areas or any changes of interest should be documented on the form.

CHECK LIST

Duties of custody officer before charge

Key Questions
Is the arrest valid and should I detain the prisoner?
Should I open a custody record?

- Release immediately if the arrest is unlawful or the detention unnecessary.

- Prisoner's rights?
    - i   Notification of named person?
    - ii Free and independent legal advice
    - iii Consult the Codes of Practice.

- Property
  Sign or refusal to sign custody record.

- Any notional arrest necessary?

- Are there reasonable grounds to believe detention necessary –

  To secure or preserve evidence?

  or

  Obtain evidence by questioning him?

- When custody record delayed and grounds for detention not explained was he:
    - i   Incapable of understanding?
    - ii Violent or likely to become violent?
    - iii In urgent need of medical attention?

- Do I need to search detainee?

- What should I seize?

- What should he retain?

- Strip search.

- Intimate search.

- Any change to property list?

46

Chapter 2
RIGHTS & ENTITLEMENTS

Whilst the preliminaries of the medical condition, the arrest and detention are considered, the prisoner's rights and entitlements should also be considered.

If in attendance, a solicitor will look towards creating a balance between the police powers and the rights of the suspect.

The solicitor will ensure the suspect knows his rights and is treated fairly in accordance with the Code. When advice is called for it may include advising the suspect to exercise his right of silence or merely helping the suspect to give an account of his actions which are under suspicion.

Rights and entitlements are an important area of the Police and Criminal Evidence Act 1984.

ACTION REGARDING RIGHTS AND ENTITLEMENTS

Q   What action must the custody officer take in respect of an arrested person's rights and entitlements?

A   In the case of all persons:

- Brought to a police station under arrest.

- Arrested at the police station, after attending there voluntarily.

And includes:

- Persons transferring from other police stations or prisons, etc.

- Persons answering to police bail.

The custody officer must:

- Inform him clearly of certain essential rights and grounds for his detention (See section 37 Police and Criminal Evidence Act 1984).

- Explain to him that he can take up his rights immediately or at any time whilst in custody.

- Give him a written notice detailing his rights and entitlements.

- Initiate without delay any arrangements to secure these rights.

- Where a delay in securing certain rights is sought or authorised, inform him of the action and the reason for it.

- Ensure the custody record is properly completed in respect of all the above actions.

C CODE 3.1	### Information to be given to arrested person verbally

Q   What information must the custody officer give to the arrested person verbally as soon as practicable?

A1   His right to have someone informed of his arrest.

C CODE 3.5	A2 His right to consult privately with a solicitor and the fact that free independent legal advice is available. (The decision should be confirmed on the custody record).

A3 His right to be allowed to read the Codes of Practice. (But he may not delay unreasonably any necessary investigations or administrative actions whilst doing so. The provision of breath, blood or urine under the terms of the Road Traffic Act 1988 need not be delayed).

A4 These rights are continuous and may be exercised immediately or at any time whilst in custody.

A5 For Commonwealth and foreign citizens the right to communicate with their High Commission, Embassy or Consulate.

C
CODE
3.3

Information to arrested person in writing

Q   What information must the custody officer give to the arrested person in writing?

C
CODE
3.2

A   He must give two written notices:

1   A Notice of Rights setting out the arrested person's rights:

- To have someone informed of his arrest. Code C 3.1(i).

- To consult privately with a solicitor. Code C 3.1(ii).

- To rec.eive free and independent legal advice. Code C 3.1(ii).

- To consult the Codes of Practice. Code C 3.1(iii).

- To a copy of the custody record. Code C 2.4.

- The prescribed caution. Code C 10.

- An explanation of how to obtain legal advice. See Code C 3.2 below.

The custody officer must give the person a written notice setting out the above, the right to a copy of the custody record in accordance with paragraph 2.4 above and the caution in the terms prescribed. The notice must also explain the arrangements for obtaining legal advice. The custody officer must also give the person an additional written notice briefly setting out his entitlement while in custody. The custody officer shall ask the person to sign the custody record to acknowledge receipt of these notices and any refusal to sign must be recorded on the custody record.

C
CODE
3A

2   A notice of entitlements while in custody, listing entitlements relating to:

- Availability of appropriate adults (see Chapter 7 on special groups). Code C 3.11, 10.6, 11.14, 16.1 and Annex A para 5 and 11(c).

- Visits. Code C 5.4.

- Contact with outside parties (including the special provisions for Commonwealth citizens and foreign nationals). Code C 5.6.

- Reasonable standards of physical comfort. Code C 8.1, 8.2 and 8.3.

- Access to toilet and washing facilities. Code C 8.4.

- Clothing. Code C 8.5.

- Adequate food and drink. Code C 8.6.

- Exercise where practicable. Code C 8.7.

- Medical attention. Code C 9.4 and 9.6.
- Provisions relating to the conduct of interviews. Code C 12.
- Suspect's right to make representation when the period of detention is reviewed. Code C 15.1.

PACE provides that translation into Welsh, the main ethnic minority languages and the principal EC languages should be available whenever they are likely to be helpful.

> C CODE 3B

It is felt that the phrase 'whenever they are likely to be helpful' means that it would not be cost effective to keep, for example, Urdu or Punjabi translations in areas where Asians are rarely encountered etc.

The custody record shall show either:

- The person's signature acknowledging the receipt of the notices, or
- Any refusal to sign the record.

> C CODE 3.2

Can a prisoner be held incommunicado

Q   Can a prisoner be held incommunicado?
A   Generally, no. The prisoner has a right not to be held incommunicado.

This right can be differentiated in four ways:

1 The police informing someone of his whereabouts, ie

- A person known to him.

- A person likely to take an interest in his welfare.

<table><tr><td>C
CODE
5.1</td></tr></table>

- This is done at public expense. If the person cannot be contacted two alternative people can be chosen. Where contact is still not made further attempts can be made at the discretion of the custody officer or the investigating officer. Custody officers are advised to consider contacting local voluntary bodies (Code 5C).

<table><tr><td>C
CODE
5.5</td></tr></table>

2 The police giving such information in response to an enquiry (subject to the person's agreement).

NOTE

In some circumstances it may not be appropriate to use the telephone to disclose information as above. See Annex B to Code C. Briefly – where a serious arrestable offence is concerned and a superintendent or above believes problems will ensue with evidence, injury, interference with persons, alerting others and hindering recovery of property, the notification can be delayed.

Also delay regarding notification may apply where drug trafficking, confiscation orders and terrorism are concerned.

3 A police-supervised visit by friends, relatives etc subject to:

<table><tr><td>C
CODE
5.4</td></tr></table>

- Availability of manpower

- Any possible hindrance to the investigation.

4 Direct access by telephone and/or letter, ie supplying the person with writing materials or allowing him to speak to **one** person by telephone for a **reasonable time**.

NOTE

<table><tr><td>C
CODE
5 A&E</td></tr></table>

The telephone call here is in addition to any communication at 1 and 2 above. An interpreter may make the telephone call or write a letter

The person must be informed that any letter or message other than to a solicitor may be read or a telephone call listened to and **may be given in evidence**. Also calls can be at public expense at the custody officer's discretion and may be terminated if abused.

C
CODE
5.7

PRESS AND PUBLIC RELATIONS OFFICE

Before disclosing information by telephone etc the custody officer should always consider the force public relations officer. Some queries by telephone will be from the press or other media sources, especially in serious or unusual cases. The investigating officer should be reminded perhaps of the necessity of formulating a press release so as to avoid confusion and disclosure of damaging information.

CUSTODY RECORD – NOTIFICATION

Must

C
CODE
5.8

- record requests and action
- record letters, messages, telephone calls and visits
- record refusal to disclose information or whereabouts

0942   Request to speak to mother Mrs Steel
0944   Allowed to speak to mother by phone
0950   Competed call
0955   Wife, Donna Steel contacted station. Prisoner refused
       to allow her to be informed of his detention.
Signed – Martin Steel

Denial or delay of rights

Q Can the custody officer deny or delay:
  1 Notifying someone of detainee's whereabouts?
  2 Giving such information in response to an enquiry?
  3 A visit?
  4 Direct access to the detainee by telephone and/or letter?

A Generally, **no**, but an officer of the rank of inspector or above
   can deny or delay direct access – 4 above (direct access). This
   can be denied or delayed on the grounds set out in Annex B,
   ie may:

C
CODE
5.6

- Interfere with evidence regarding an arrestable
  offence or a serious arrestable offence; or

- Interfere with person or cause physical injury to
  other; or

- Alert others suspected of said offence; or

- Hinder recovery of property obtained from such an
  offence; or if

- The arrestable offence or serious arrestable offence is
  drugs trafficking or one involving confiscation orders;
  or

- Either of consequences set out in paragraph 8 of
  Annex B and terrorism are involved.

Some confusion has arisen as to whether this denial or delay only
applies when serious arrestable offences are involved. The way
we read the code is that the inspector or above can deny or delay
a letter and/or a telephone call merely for arrestable offences
provided the grounds set out above apply.

Therefore an inspector or above can only deny or delay direct
access via a telephone call and/or a letter but see Annex B
paragraph 1 and 2 in total where a superintendent can delay, ie
delay but not deny, the right to notify of arrest or allow access to
legal advice.

This area has now been clarified by the addition to Code 5.6 that
for this purpose 'any reference to a SAO in Annex B, includes an
AO'.

Right to legal advice

Q *What is the prisoner's right to legal advice?*
A Generally any person may at any time consult and communicate, **privately**, in person, in writing or by telephone with a free, independent legal advisor. The custody officer must inform him of this right.

C
CODE
6.1

Legal Advice Formula

The person concerned must be told he has a

* Right to FREE and INDEPENDENT legal advice and asked if he wants such advice. [The custody officer should make every effort to secure a specific legal advisor, or duty solicitor for the detainee. Further guidance is given in Note 6B]

C
CODE
6.5

If the person declines to speak to a solicitor

- Right to speak to a solicitor on the telephone and asked if he wishes to do so [This conversation should be in PRIVATE, unless the geography of the custody suite makes this impractical.]

NOTE ONE
The explanation of both aspects of this right must be recorded together with the detainees choices.

NOTE TWO
When a person declines these rights he should be asked the reason and any reason recorded. (Once the detainee has clearly declined both the above, they should not be pressed for their reasons)

NOTE THREE
Delay only per Annex B. Otherwise, without delay secure legal advice. Prominently displayed poster advertising legal advice should be at every charging area of every police station in English and other languages appropriate to the area.

C
CODE
6.4

No attempt should be made to dissuade the suspect from obtaining legal advice. Reminders of the right to free legal advice must be given.

- Initial action. C 3.5
- Immediately prior to interview by the interviewing officer. Code C 11.2
- Before conducting a review of detention by the review officer, who should also record same in the custody record. Code C 15.3
- Charging. C 16.4 & 16.5
- Before identification by parade, group or video by the identification officer. Code D 2.15 (ii)
- Before any intimate body sample is taken. This should be recorded in the custody record. Code D 5.2

To further emphasise this important area of **rights** we will examine them from another angle. That of when to **stop** or **delay** these rights. Mention has already been made of the inspector or above denying or delaying a telephone call and/or letter. We will now look at a superintendent or above.

STOPPING OR DELAYING RIGHTS

Q When can I delay the right to legal advice or not to be held incommunicado?

A A custody officer cannot, but both or either can be delayed when detained for a serious arrestable offence not yet charged with an offence and a superintendent or above has reasonable grounds to believe that it will interfere with or harm evidence connected with serious arrestable offence or interfere with or lead to physical injury to other persons or will alert other persons suspected of having committed such offence or will hinder recovery of property obtained as result of such offence.

> C
> CODE
> Annex B

NOTE ONE

These rights may also be delayed where a serious arrestable offence and officer has reasonable grounds for believing:

- A drug trafficking offence which has benefited suspect and recovery will be hindered; or

- An offence concerning a confiscation order which has benefited the suspect and recovery will be hindered.

NOTE TWO

An inspector or above can delay the right to direct access, ie the right to contact someone personally, in similar circumstances to the way in which a superintendent delays the right to legal advice or incommunicado (no one told of the detention).

> C
> CODE
> 5.6

How long can we delay these rights?

Q How long can the superintendent delay these rights?

A Only as long as is necessary and in no case beyond 36 hours, or 48 hours regarding terrorism.

NOTE

That where the above grounds cease to apply the person must be asked if he now wants to exercise his right not to remain incommunicado and to legal advice.

The custody records must be noted accordingly.

Q   Who can give legal advice under PACE.?
A •   A solicitor

C
CODE
6.12

[Holding a current practice certificate]

• A trainee solicitor

• A duty solicitor representative

• An accredited representative

[Held on the Legal Aid Board Register]

• A non-accredited or probationer representative

NOTE ONE

All the above can give legal advice, however an inspector or above, can refuse to admit probationer or non-accredited representatives only, when the officer considers their presence might hinder the investigation. Once admitted, all the above are subject to paragraphs 6.6 - 6.10 (Code C) in relation to interviews.

NOTE TWO

Where the same solicitor acts for more than one client he may have a conflict of interests if the clients', cases are connected. He may directly or inadvertently pass information from one to the other.

C
CODE
ANNEX B
NOTE B 4

Access to a specific solicitor may be delayed where there are reasonable grounds to believe that, inadvertently or otherwise, a message will be passed on or that the solicitor will act in some other way so as to bring about interference with evidence, persons or property etc as above.

C
CODE
ANNEX B

The delay of notification of arrest of a person does not automatically mean that the delay of legal advice should follow.

In practice, a solicitor's clerk is quite a common encounter. The custody officer should make sure the clerk is properly accredited to the firm as it is important that the suspect receives the correct legal advice. This is even more important when establishing the status of probationary or non-accredited representatives and the Code of Practice gives further advice.

> C
> CODE
> 6.13 & 6.14

IMPORTANT RECAP ON RIGHTS AND ENTITLEMENTS WHEN CAN THEY BE DENIED OR DELAYED?

Checklist

Right not to be held incommunicado and the right to legal advice

> C
> CODE
> 5 & 6

Q When do these rights apply?
A On arrival at the police station.

Q Can they be stopped?
A No.

Q Can they be delayed?
A Yes - for up to 36 hours (48 hours for terrorism).

Q Who can delay them?
A Superintendent or above for legal advice or incommunicado or inspector or above for direct access.

Q On what grounds can they be delayed?
A When detained for a serious arrestable offence with reasonable grounds to believe:

- Interfere with or harm evidence of serious arrestable offence.

- Interfere with or physical injury to other persons.

- Alert other persons suspected of having committed such offence.

- Will hinder recovery of property obtained as result of such offence.

- Drug trafficking offence.

- Offence concerning a confiscation order, etc.

If any of the above grounds cease to apply, the rights should be given immediately.

Right to consult the Codes of Practice and the right to a copy of the custody record

C
CODE
2.4 & 3.1

Q When do these rights apply?
A On arrival at the police station for the Codes and any time within 12 months of release for a copy.

Q Can they be stopped?
A No. So long as the detainee does not delay unreasonably any necessary investigative or administrative action by consulting the Codes.

Right to direct access

C
CODE
5.4 & 5.6

Q *What is direct access?*
A When a friend, relative or solicitor visits the suspect or has a telephone conversation with the suspect or the suspect is allowed to send a letter.

Q *Can direct access be delayed?*
A The custody officer has a discretion regarding visits. He should allow visits where possible in the light of available manpower and possible hindrance to the investigation.

Otherwise an inspector or above can deny or delay a letter or telephone conversation under Code C Annex B, though this is extended to include arrestable as well as serious arrestable offences.

DELAYING THE RIGHT TO HAVE SOMEONE INFORMED OF THE WHEREABOUTS OF A PRISONER TO ENABLE A SUCCESSFUL HOUSE SEARCH TO TAKE PLACE

Q *Can the right be delayed to facilitate a house search?*
A It may be tempting to so delay in order to recover stolen property, evidence etc. Nevertheless, no such delay is permitted under PACE, except where detained in connection with a SAO and a superintendent or above under Code C 5.6 and Annex B considers that to exercise the right would hinder the recovery of property obtained as a result of such an offence.

NOTE ONE

Where the detention is not in connection with a serious arrestable offence then it appears the legislators intended the risk of losing evidence and stolen property. Notification cannot be delayed in these circumstances.

In some circumstances an officer could be sent to an address where a search is to be made and also where the person lives who is to be notified of the detention. A search and notification could be made together to avoid evidence being removed etc.

Under section 18(1) PACE a constable may enter and search any premises occupied or controlled by a person who is under arrest for an arrestable offence if reasonable grounds for suspecting that there is evidence on the premises relating to that offence or to some other arrestable offence connected with or similar to that offence.

Normally an Inspector or above needs to authorise such a search in writing BUT where the search is made before taking the person to a police station and obtaining an authorisation from the inspector or above then the presence of that person at a place other than a police station is necessary for the effective investigation of the offence AND the constable shall inform the inspector or above of the search as soon as possible after it has been made.

NOTE TWO

PACE
S 18 (8)

The inspector or above who authorises, or is informed of, such a search shall record the grounds and object of the search. Where the detainee is at a police station when this record is made it shall be included in the custody record.

The above **rights and entitlements** have caused and will continue to cause some headaches for the custody officer.

VISITS

If the suspect needs to get a message to an accomplice it is only natural that friends, relatives and even solicitors will become willing, unwilling or unknowing carriers of such messages. Your force standing orders or guidelines should cover what to do.

Visits are at the custody officer's discretion. Generally visits will only be allowed if the officer in the case has no objections. Unless the officer in the case requests otherwise a visit will be within the sight but out of hearing of the police. If thought necessary an officer may be present within sight and hearing throughout a visit of even the spouse, but not a solicitor. Again depending on your own force procedures a visit is best made out of the cell, but if nowhere else is available a cell may be used.

Be aware of the repercussions from allowing the investigating officer to be present at visits. It could lead to pressures being exerted by the investigating officer or allegations of the same and of the visit being regarded as an interview.

Visits by police officers should **all** be recorded whether made to perform hourly or half hourly checks or for some other reason. Precise times should be used. See next chapter for treatment of prisoner.

CONTACT WITH OUTSIDE PARTIES

See the access to friends, relatives, solicitors etc personally or by telephone or letter, which is dealt with earlier in this chapter.

When solicitors, friends etc visit the detainee be on the lookout for hand-held tape recorders and mobile telephones. If you suspect the detainee might use the telephone from his cell or elsewhere ask for it to be left in the charge office before allowing the visit.

Foreign nationals are dealt with later at Chapter 7.

Chapter 3
TREATMENT

The key to professionalism is to initiate and maintain Good Practice with care and custody.

CONDITIONS OF DETENTION

This is a vital area often neglected due to its mundane nature. It is sometimes the Achilles heel of a good custody officer.

This area is a source of minor complaints associated with a complaint of a more substantial nature, with the custody officer being a hostage of fortune.

Canteen culture – give 'em nothing. The custody officer's professionalism rises above canteen culture. Treat a person with respect and hopefully respect will be returned.

GOOD PRACTICE

Complete and **accurate records** lead to less likelihood of a successful complaint.

Know the discretionary and mandatory aspects of care and custody. Failure to grant an entitlement under the Code must be justified. It must be **fully recorded** in the custody record.

SUBSTANTIATE DECISIONS

In reality there are valid reasons to substantiate the custody officer's decisions, unfortunately they are sometimes absent from the custody record.

Behaviour breeds behaviour – the way a prisoner is initially treated affects the way he responds to custody staff and any interviewing.

Firm but fair – always calm, always patient, always reasonable.

PARENT LEGISLATION GOVERNING TREATMENT

PACE
S 39(1)

Responsibilities in relation to **ALL** persons detained.

PACE section 39(1) states it shall be the duty of the custody officer at a police station to ensure:

- That all persons in police detention at the station are treated in accordance with this Act and any Code of Practice issued under it and relating to the treatment of persons in police detention; and

- That all matters relating to such persons which are required by this Act or by such Codes of Practice to be recorded are recorded in the custody records relating to such persons.

TREATMENT PROCEDURES SIMPLIFIED
(The overall picture of Chapter 3)

Mandatory	Heating, lighting, ventilation of cells	Code 8.2
Discretionary	Cell occupancy	Code 8.1
Mandatory	Restraints (handcuffs only)	Code 8.2
Discretionary	Use of handcuffs in cell	Code 8.2
Mandatory	Access to toilet and washing facilities	Code 8.4
Discretionary	Blankets, mattresses, pillows	Code 8.3
Mandatory	Provide replacement clothing	Code 8.5
Discretionary	Removing clothing for investigation, hygiene, health or cleansing	Code 8.5
Mandatory	Two light meals and one main meal	Code 8.6
Discretionary	Drinks between meals	Code 8.6
Mandatory	Offer varied diet. Meet special dietary needs or religious requirements (as far as practicable)	Code 8.6
Discretionary	Meals supplied by friends or relatives	Code 8.6
Discretionary	Reasonable force	Code 8.9
Mandatory	Brief outdoor exercise (if practicable)	Code 8.7
Discretionary	Supervisory visits each hour, drunken person at least every half hour	Code 8.10
Discretionary	Juveniles and others at risk should be visited more frequently	Code 8A
Mandatory	Record any minor injuries or ailments	Code9.A
Mandatory	Obtain medical assistance for persons in need of medical attention	Code 9.2
Discretionary	Minor ailments or injury: medical attention not required	Code9.A
Mandatory	Person suffering from head injuries – call police surgeon when in doubt	Code9.B
Mandatory	Isolate persons suffering from a significant infectious disease	Code 9.3
Mandatory	Call a police surgeon upon request	

	for a medical examination	Code 9.4
Mandatory	Responsible for safeguarding and ensuring detainee given the opportunity to take or apply medication	Code 9.5
Mandatory	Obtain advice of police surgeon for persons having medication or claiming to require medication for a serious or potentially serious medical condition	Code 9.6
Mandatory	Report complaint re treatment to inspector if made by or on behalf of detainee or if it comes to the notice of any officer	Code 9.1
Mandatory	Call a police surgeon if complaint relates to assault or unnecessary unreasonable force	Code 9.1

CELLS

As far as practicable, not more than **one** person shall be detained in **each** cell.

Your force orders may differ slightly, but generally:

- Cells should not be used as a matter of routine. Consider **other secure places** of detention.

- When considering placing a prisoner in a cell the custody officer should be satisfied that the detainee is in **a fit condition**. (A medical checklist appears post).

- Prisoners presenting an **exceptional risk** such as potential suicide cases or escapees should be catered for by the custody officer. Check your force orders regarding the use of the form POL 1 Exceptional risk prisoner form.

- When **one to a cell** is not practicable consider moving to another police station. Never mix sexes or place juveniles with adults, except mother and child etc. Take into account the relationship between the adult and child, the availability of a suitable adult to mind the child and the use of social services, if necessary. It is suggested that one or three to a cell is better than two. In practice the third prisoner acts as a restraining influence and could be a witness or raise the alarm. Prisoners held at at police stations on behalf of HM Prisons (eg prison officer strike) should never be mixed with 'police' prisoners.

- See Chapter 7 for juveniles in cells.

CUSTODY RECORD – CELL DETAILS

Advise to:

- Record time placed in cell
- Record which room if not a cell
- Record if more than one prisoner
- Record prisoners' names or reference numbers who were sharing the cell
- State reason for sharing

1830 hours – Placed Mr Head in cell number two with Mr Bingham (Ref 4/92). Other two cells were full.

MEDICAL CHECK LIST

Visual matters
- Is prisoner bleeding anywhere?
- Any broken bones or teeth?
- Other adverse signs - bruises, sores, swollen areas or rash?
- Needle marks of drug takers?
- Signs of mental disorder, amnesia, concussion?
- Any medic alert necklace, bracelet, card etc?
- Check general condition – agitated, sweating, pale or weak etc.
- Difficulty breathing, nausea, vomiting, dizziness, coughing blood or blood in motions or urine?

Non-visual matters
- When and why did he last see a doctor?
- Any recent or serious injury or illness?
- Any tablets/medicine etc? Check with doctor if necessary
- Any recurring illness eg diabetes or epilepsy?
- Any contagious matter, eg AIDS, hepatitis, measles, mumps etc?

Apparent drunkenness

- Does he smell of alcohol?
- Be concerned if breathing irregular, noisy or faint
- Any medic alert necklace, bracelet or card?
- Any visible signs of injury?
- Any unusual signs or symptoms?

NOTE

Any head injuries even those of a minor nature should be referred to a medical practitioner

HEATING

Cells in use must be adequately heated, cleaned and ventilated.

- A recent case concerning **hunt saboteurs** highlighted a complaint of inadequate **heating** in a cell during their detention.
- The custody officer should monitor the rise and fall of temperature to ensure reasonable conditions for the prisoner.

- Cells should be checked for **cleanliness** before and after each prisoner. If any damage is found then an entry should be made on the custody record of the prisoner concerned. Evidence of damage should be obtained by a scenes of crime officer or a polaroid camera. Also a check for instruments to effect an escape or injury is essential. Cell blocks should be subjected to regular checks by officers properly equipped with ladders and lights for a thorough search of each cell.

Remember prisoners often defecate or urinate in their cells. This is sometimes caused by ignoring their bell-push or calls.

- **Emergency call buttons** in cells should be checked daily. Some buttons can be switched off when drunk or obnoxious prisoners are in custody. These buttons are for the protection of both the prisoner and the custody officer and a certain amount of annoyance must be borne by the custody officer. When the button is out of order then visits at 15 minutes intervals are suggested. When a bell is pushed avoid shouting 'what do you want?' This infuriates some prisoners and the personal touch is always better.

LIGHTING/PHYSICAL RESTRAINTS

C
CODE
8.2

Cells must be adequately lit, subject to such dimming as is compatible with safety and security to allow persons detained overnight to sleep.

- Common sense and fairness must prevail. If a prisoner is unpredictable or of exceptional risk it may be wise to leave the **light** on to watch the prisoner's moves. Otherwise sensible, fair use of lights is called for.

- **No additional restraints** should be used within a locked cell unless absolutely necessary, and then only suitable handcuffs.

- **Handcuffs** – guidance in the use of handcuffs is given in HO Circular 62/1992 which gives the considerations as:

the safety of the police and public

the safety and security of prisoners

Officers must have reasonable grounds to believe that the prisoner will use violence or attempt escape. They should only be used in exceptional circumstances on juveniles, women or elderly prisoners.

- **'Flexicuffs'** can be used in emergencies when time is of the essence, eg a large number of arrests. They should not be used routinely, for long periods, or be overtightened, and remember they require cutting equipment to be at hand.

- **Rigid handcuffs** are appearing throughout the country combining the restraint of the old style cuffs with an element of control, hence the need to traine officers. We suggest that they should not be used to secure prisoners together in a daisy chain, or to handcuff prisoners to police officers, as the stronger individual could be dangerous to the other. Custody officers need to be aware of their force policy in relation to handcuffs.

- **Handcuff restraint** can be useful, to save injury to staff or the prisoner injuring himself. Problems arise with hand or wrist injury to prisoners or custody staff trapping their fingers etc. Some prisoners will struggle violently to avoid handcuffs.

CUSTODY RECORD – HANDCUFFS

If handcuffs used: (advise)
- Record use
- Person authorising
- Record reason
- Time restraint applied
- Time removed
- Record any marks or injuries to any party

2045	Handcuffs applied to prisoner. Authorised by self because of person's fighting drunk state. He attempts to strike out at custody staff at every opportunity - shouting obscenities and threatening everybody.
2348	Handcuffs removed. Prisoner now calm, but still abusive. Minor swelling and abrasions to both wrists - minor injuries and I feel no medical aid needed. No other injuries.

BEDDING

Blankets, mattresses, pillows and other bedding supplied should be of a reasonable standard and in a clean and sanitary condition.

- Do not issue as a matter of **routine**. Only when an overnight stop is necessary, or the prisoner's condition or lack of clothing warrants it.

- Check the **condition** of bedding after use and consider offences of **criminal damage** if necessary. If soiled by bodily fluids etc consider destroying by burning. Launder after use in most cases.

- Two good reasons for **not touching** prisoners' **blankets** – one, for your own protection from their bodily fluids and two, your uniform becomes covered in blanket fluff. The prisoner should place his blankets in the laundry bag.

- Note any **refusal** to issue, eg to drunks or any damage to bedding together with action taken if any.

NOTE
Code C Note 8B states the above is important for persons detained under terrorist or immigration law or others who may stay in police custody longer.

WASHING ETC

Access to toilet and washing facilities must be provided.

- Ensure sufficient **supplies** of disposable toiletries.

- Never leave prisoner **alone** with such articles.

- Follow force practice but generally only allow one prisoner **out of a cell** at any one time and have an officer in attendance.

- Don't allow **sharp objects**, chairs, rubbish etc to collect in showers/washing areas as these have been used as weapons or taken back to cells for future use.

- **Shaving** facilities are at the custody officer's discretion. A plastic disposable safety razor should be used with shaving foam.

- Always wear **gloves** when handling razors.

- **Dispose** of razors in sealed containers, never in waste paper baskets.

- Allow a prisoner to **wash** prior to a **court appearance**.

- Any **refusal** of above or other unusual event should be recorded on the custody record.

CUSTODY RECORD – TOILETS ETC

Advise to record

- Record access to toilets/washing facilities

- Any requests by the prisoner

- Any denial or refusal

- If denied, reason and person denying prisoner access to be recorded

0830   Denied access to washing facilities. Prisoner remains violent and abusive attempting to attack any custody staff approaching him.

        P.H. PS 457

Clothing

If it is necessary to remove a person's clothes, clothing for investigation, hygiene or health reasons, or for cleaning, adequate replacements shall be provided. A person may not be interviewed unless such clothing has been provided.

| C CODE 8.5 |

- A number of forces **replace clothing** with yellow or white paper body suits and socks in the absence of alternative clothing. A blanket may be necessary to supplement a paper suit on cold days.

- Every effort should be made to obtain **alternative clothing** for a court appearance. Courts frown upon persons appearing in police issue body suits. A prisoner is not normally interviewed in a body suit.

- The **removal of clothing**, if not done by a scenes of crime officer or a forensic scientist, normally falls to the custody office staff. Suitable training should be given regarding the protection of oneself, the contamination of evidence; the preservation and correct packaging of evidence.

- Always **record** what has been done and give a statement for continuity to produce the clothing as an exhibit if pertinent. Custody staff are good at this stage as:

    - Not involved in the case.

    - Not been to scene of crime re contamination of evidence and

    - Could have a better attitude.

- When retaining clothing for **safety reasons** the more information available the better. Some custody officers remove shoe laces but leave trousers with sharp zips. Some remove shoes, belts and jackets as a matter of course. But each case has to be judged on its merits and retention explained in the custody record. A consensus or policy is good practice.

- Thoroughly check all clothing brought in. Ideally it should be recorded in depth to help the investigation and safeguard against allegations of clothing being lost or stolen.

The custody officer may seize clothes and personal effects, where he believes the person may:

PACE
S 54

- **Cause injury to himself or others** eg ties, belts, zips, shoes, keys

- **Damage property** eg shoes, matches, lighter

- **Interfere with evidence** eg money, portable telephone

- **Assist him to escape** eg keys, shoes, or

- **That they may be evidence of or relating to an offence**

NOTE

When items are brought to a police station for a prisoner they should be handed to the custody officer who, after examination, can use his discretion whether to give to the prisoner. All actions should be recorded in the custody record.

CUSTODY RECORD – CLOTHING

Must	• Record any replacement clothing offered
Advise to record	• Circumstances of the removal and offer of replacement
	• Time
	• Person authorising removal
	• Person removing
	• Person present
	• Article removed, colour, material, make etc
	• Disposal and reference number – eg forensic HOLAB number if sent for examination
	• Replacement clothing offered
	• Any request by prisoner
	• Any arrangements made for obtaining permanent replacement.

0930	Authorised to remove all clothing for forensic examination by myself. All clothing removed by prisoner and handed to PC 5 Atidor in the presence of myself. (Exhibit RA 1-7 HOLAB 69/92) Given white paper overalls. Officer in charge is arranging for replacement clothing for 1200 hours today, prior to interview.

FOOD / DRINK / DIETS

Food in any period of 24 hours

C
CODE
8.6

- **One main meal and**
- **Two light meals should be offered at police expense.**

These are normally obtained from police canteens where available or from local cafes or restaurants.

Also family and friends can supply meals at the prisoner's or their expense.

Meals should be offered at usual meal times where practicable.

C
CODE
8.C

Drink

- **Supply at all meal times**
- **Supply at reasonable intervals between meal times**
- These will be water, tea or coffee or something similar. On no account must alcohol be supplied or any other drink which could be alleged to have 'loosened the prisoner's tongue'

81

Diet

- **When necessary, advice should be sought from a police surgeon on medical or dietary matters.**

- **As far as practicable, meals should:**

  i   **be varied in diet**
  ii **meet special dietary needs**
  iii **meet religious beliefs.**

  eg avoid certain meat and animals which are slaughtered in certain ways for persons of the Jewish or Muslim faiths.

NOTE

Code C 8B regarding these provisions being particularly important for those detained under terrorism law for long periods.

Other points of interest

1 Meals supplied by **family or friends** can upset other prisoners and provoke **jealousies**.

2 Consider the interviewing officers' wishes but feed **prior to interview** if possible. This minimises complaints of being kept without food. There is no way of telling how long an interview will take.

3 **Check** everything brought in and remember that the ingenuity of people is designed to defeat your search. Be aware of goods, apparently sealed by the manufacturer as these could have been tampered with.

4 Do not **punish all** for the wrongdoing of a few.

5   Look at **each prisoner's needs**, as they may not have eaten for a long period and an extra meal might be necessary. Normally fixed mealtimes are followed which fit into police and court-times and shift patterns eg 0800 breakfast, 1200 lunch and 1800 dinner/tea.

6   Have a list of **acceptable meals** which can be supplied by friends and relatives, eg no canned drinks or drinks in glass bottles, meals to be of reasonable quantity (otherwise custody staff will be searching food parcels for long periods).

7   Certain officers and police civilian staff have faced disciplinary proceedings for **eating prisoners' food** which had been declined by the prisoner. This is an area where the custody officer should supervise closely.

8   Plates, cups, knives and forks etc are usually plastic for reasons of **safety** of the prisoners and the police.

Police pot cups have been given to prisoners and police staff have used prisoners' plastic cups after use by prisoners with obvious **dangers**.

9   **Remand prisoners** will demand certain items such as **beer** quoting such things as 'prison remand rules'. HM Prison rules do not apply to remand to police cells.

10 **Remove** all remnants of meals and cutlery and plates promptly.

11 **Record** all refusals or other matters regarding meals.

NOTE

Code C 8B highlights the importance of a varied diet for person detained under terrorist or immigration law, or others who may stay in police custody longer.

CUSTODY RECORD – FOOD	
Must	• Record all meals offered
Advise	• Record any requests
	• Record any special provisions
	• Record denials or refusals
	• Record reasons for any of the above

> 1230   PC 5 R Atidor offered hot meal (fish and chips) and a hot drink (tea). Prisoner abusive and threatened to throw the food over the officer. Hot drink placed on open cell hatch, but thrown into corridor by the prisoner. All meal refused and disposed of in dustbin.
>
> PH PS 457

C CODE 8.7

EXERCISE

Brief outdoor exercise shall be offered daily if practicable.

Exercise depends on:

- The **duration** in the cells;

- **Weather conditions** where no indoor facilities; and

- His personal wishes.

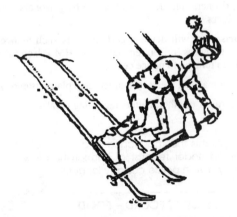

The number of prisoners to be exercised collectively will be determined by how **secure** the exercise area is, the number of officers available for **escort** and the potential for violence or escape of the prisoners.

Always **check** exercise yard or area before each session for breaks in security netting etc or for objects and weapons etc.

Never let prisoners exercise **alone** and be aware of **exceptional risk** prisoners.

Periods of exercise depend on custody officer's **discretion**. Normally two daily periods of 30 minutes each.

Do not allow **communication** between those jointly charged etc or between those where communication is undesirable.

Don't look on it as a chore as the custody staff can also get some **benefit**, fresh air, relaxation.

Be aware of **safety** risks both to police officers and prisoners eg if icy, sand and salt should be used.

One officer to one prisoner or, if placid, old or infirm, one officer to two prisoners may suffice.

CUSTODY RECORD – EXERCISE

Advise to
- Record any requests
- Record any exercise offered or denied
- Any period of exercise given
- Any occurrences during exercise eg sprained ankle
- Officer supervising or denying exercise and reason eg icy conditions

1000   PS Paul Harper 457 offered individual exercise period for 15 minutes. Prisoner wanted to exercise with co-accused. Denied by DC N Smith, officer in case, for reasons of contamination of evidence etc.

REASONABLE FORCE

Reasonable force may be used for the following purposes:
- **To secure compliance with reasonable instructions including instructions given in pursuance of a Code of Practice.**
- **To prevent escape, injury, damage to property or the destruction of evidence.**

C
CODE
8.9

All custody staff should be trained in **restraint techniques,** and be suitably clad for violent prisoners, eg wear jacket and gloves if known to bite

PLAN, PREPARE AND ACT

- Have enough staff present to deal with a violent prisoner, eg one to the head, one officer on each limb.
- In practice there are usually insufficient officers and injuries occur.

Explain to other prisoners the reasons for the noise and shouting etc to calm their fears.

Secure all other prisoners first before attempting to deal with a violent prisoner.

CUSTODY RECORD – REASONABLE FORCE

Advise to
- Record reasonable force used
- Record instructions to officer to use reasonable force. **or** what we are using reasonable force to prevent –
  Escape
  Injury
  Damage
  Destruction of evidence

09.30   PS 456 P.Harper requested the prisoner to leave his cell for a court attendance. He refused to leave and became violent and abusive. The custody officer PS57 Calligan authorised PC5 Raymond Atidor to forcibly remove the prisoner from his cell. We each took hold of an arm and dragged him outside the police station to the escort vehicle. There were no discernable injuries.

SUPERVISORY VISITS

Persons detained should be visited every hour.

C CODE 8.10

- Those who are drunk every half hour, and should be roused and spoken to on each visit.
- Where possible juveniles and others at risk should be visited more regularly (Note 8.A).
- Should the custody officer feel concerned about a person, he should obtain medical treatment.

C CODE 12.2

- Speaking to or rousing the prisoner does not count as an interruption of an 8 hour period of rest.

i   record the need for any **special** supervisory visits and enhance the entry with a highlighter to make sure visits stand out for quick reference.

ii   staff should have **matches and lighters** (preferably lighters) to provide prisoners with lights for cigarettes. It may be prudent to save staff time by restricting the provision of lights to hourly visits. The giving of all lights should be recorded.

iii **all visits to be recorded** as soon as possible thereafter. The state of the prisoner should also be recorded especially if drunk, eg asleep, still drunk, very active (drug withdrawal) or threatening staff etc.

iv when doing a supervisory visit an officer should **not enter a cell** containing two or more prisoners unless there is another officer at the door of the cell. It is not sufficient to look at a drunken person or those at special visits. They should be spoken to or physically roused and checked.

v   where a person is charged with murder or other serious or degrading offence a **continuous watch** should be kept.

On a scale of priorities, visits rank pretty high. Deaths in custody normally call for a thorough examination of visit records.

CUSTODY RECORD – SUPERVISORY VISITS

Advise to
- Record any special instructions
- Record the reason for the visit
- Authorising officer
- Time of visit
- Condition/demeanour
- Record any action taken

0230   PS 456 Paul Harper hourly visit. Prisoner awake given drink of water and lights in cell put fully on at his request.

TREATMENT OF DETAINED PERSONS

The police do not receive medical training other than first aid in most cases. It is the common sense and conscientiousness of officers that prevent more deaths in custody than actually occur.

This is a life and death area and great importance should be given to it.

Medical treatment

C
CODE
9.2

The custody officer must immediately call the police surgeon (or, in urgent cases, eg where the person does not show signs of sensibility or awareness, send the person to hospital or call the nearest available medical practitioner) if a person brought to a police station or already detained there:

- Appears to be suffering from physical illness or a mental disorder; or
- Is injured; or
- Fails to respond normally to questions or conversation (other than through drunkenness alone); or
- Otherwise appears to need medical attention.

This applies even if the person makes no request for medical attention and whether or not he has recently had medical treatment elsewhere (unless brought to the police station direct from hospital).

It is not intended that the contents of this paragraph should delay the transfer of a person to a place of safety under section 136 of the Mental Health Act 1983 where that is applicable. Where an assessment under that Act is to take place at the police station, the custody officer has discretion not to call the police surgeon so long as he believes that the assessment by a registered medical practitioner can be undertaken without undue delay.

A police surgeon does not need to be called for minor ailments or injuries which do not need attention. However, they must be recorded and if in doubt call the police surgeon.

C
CODE
9A

- Similar to Chapter 1 on initial detention, **full records** must be made of injuries, illness, medication, requests, etc.

- If in doubt, safety first and call a **police surgeon.**

CUSTODY RECORD – FOR CALLING A SURGEON

Advise to
- Record reason for request
- Record person contacted
- Full record of advice given
- Action taken

Example

Prisoner states he is suffering from the following symptoms which are not visible: ie pains in the chest, shortage of breath and anxiety but has no history of heart disease. Police surgeon, Dr Who, contacted who advised that the prisoner be sent to hospital by ambulance. Ambulance contacted and attending in 10 minutes.

CUSTODY RECORD – WHEN INJURED BUT NO SURGEON

Must
- Record all injuries and minor ailments

Advise to
- Record how injury acquired
- Fully record action taken

Example

One centimetre gash on bridge of nose caused by falling down prior to arrest and hitting nose on wall. Elastoplast used to stop bleeding. Prisoner and myself satisfied with treatment. No surgeon called, (ask prisoner to sign).

- **Property** and **speech** of prisoner give clues as to the medical condition

- It is important to remember that a person who appears to be drunk or behaving abnormally may be suffering from illness or the effects of drugs or may have sustained injury (particularly head injury) which is not apparent, and that someone needing or addicted to certain drugs may experience harmful effects within a short time of being deprived of their supply. Police should therefore always call the police surgeon when in any doubt, and act with all due speed.

- Persons apparently drunk with injuries to the head, however minor, should be referred for medical advice.

- Persons who appear drunk or drugged should be placed in the recovery position or three-quarters prone position, ie laid on one side with mouth open. This allows any vomit to exit the mouth and keeps the airways free.

- **Prior to** contacting the police surgeon obtain:

    i   full list of injuries and overall symptoms

    ii   name of own doctor

    iii medication taken

    iv general history from PNC re drugs etc

    v   relevant attendant circumstances, ie first time arrested, or appears to be anxious and/or claims angina pains.

- Consider speaking to prisoner's **own doctor** with his permission. Record all medical history relevant and doctor's closeness to prisoner, eg is he the family doctor?

- If prisoner goes to **hospital** consider:

    i   unconditional release

    ii   bail

    iii supply escort if necessary

    iv send any medication from his property

    v   full record to be made.

- If the prisoner is taken to a medical practitioner consider:

    i   check surgery for dangerous objects and escape routes

    ii   arrange and brief the escorting officer in

91

consultation with the medical practitioner, ie as to whether the officer should remain during the examination or stand nearby.

    iii obtain information relevant to the prisoner and brief the medical practitioner. This information to be obtained from:

- person's own GP
- dispensary chemist
- friends/relatives
- prisoner himself
- prisoner's property
- PNC/local intelligence.

    iv Always brief the medical practitioner regarding the prisoner's overall demeanour.

CUSTODY RECORD – MEDICAL ADVICE

Advise to
- Record incident fully ie injuries, symptoms etc
- Record action taken ie treatment, advice
- Examination
- Record outcome ie fit for detention/interview

1830	Prisoner keeps banging his head on cell door causing minor abrasions to forehead with a deep cut on left eyebrow. Police surgeon Mr Bainbridge called at the police station to see another prisoner and I asked him to examine the cut eye.
	Advised to give prisoner one tablet every 4 hours to calm him down. Doctor injected prisoner in arm and applied a dressing to eye wound. Prisoner much quieter on doctor's departure. Doctor stated fit for detention and fit for interview.

INFECTIOUS DISEASES

If the custody officer is told, or feels, that a person at a police station under arrest has an infectious disease he must isolate the person and his property until he has obtained medical advice.

C
CODE
9.3

Example

A female prostitute is detained. She looks pale and complains of nausea. She struggled violently with four officers, spitting and biting and scratching them.

She has drug user's equipment in her handbag. It is suspected she has AIDS, or hepatitis B.

- Isolate person and property.

- Contact the police surgeon for advice.

- Identify the officers concerned and advise them to contact the police surgeon, submit 'injury on duty' forms where applicable.

- Precautions to continue while in custody or until tests prove negative.

- The cell will be cleared and bedding dealt with as advised by the police surgeon or as laid down in force orders.

- Diseases to watch for include measles, mumps, chicken pox, venereal disease, hepatitis B and AIDS.

- High risk groups for AIDS include: homosexuals, drug users and prostitutes.

- If in doubt consult a police surgeon.

VERMINOUS PRISONERS

Many tramps or persons living in squalid conditions will have **body lice or fleas** etc which can easily contaminate custody staff or other prisoners.

Most local authorities provide a **cleaning service**. Clothes and towels etc may need destroying together with any police blankets or bedding.

Cells, police vehicles and other areas used by the prisoner may need **fumigation**.

If the prisoner refuse to be cleaned, then the local authority will be asked to apply to a magistrates' court for **an order to use** force under the Public Health Act.

"I request a medical examination"

- The police **must** call a **surgeon** in these circumstances.
- If the police surgeon **refuses to attend** then record same and contact another police surgeon or medical practitioner. Any problems with a particular surgeon should be reported to a senior officer.

C
CODE
9.4

- If a medical practitioner does not **record** his **clinical findings** in the custody record the record must show where they are recorded.
- The detainee may be examined by a medical practitioner of his own choosing but must pay any fee himself.

CUSTODY RECORD – REQUEST FOR MEDICAL EXAMINATION

Must	• Record any request for a medical examination • Record any arrangements made • Record any medical directions
Advise to	• Record any observations or relevant information • Record details of examination • Place • Physician attending • Escort/person present • Place record made if not made in custody record • Record the present and future state of the prisoner ie fit for detention – fit for an interview • Any subsequent examination by the prisoner's own doctor

09.50 Requested a medical examination stating that he feels dizzy. Appears pale and sweaty. Police surgeon Bainbridge contacted and will attend the prisoner in half an hour. He did not give me any medical directions.

10.20 Examination in police station surgery by Dr Bainbridge where PC Hellawell, the escorting officer, remained outside the surgery at the doctor's request. Record of the examination retained by the doctor. The doctor said he was fit for detention and interview. Medical direction to give prisoner one x paracetamol every four hours.

MEDICATION

If a person is required to take or apply any previously prescribed medication in compliance with medical directions:

C
CODE
9.5

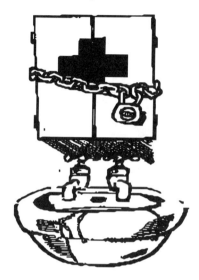

- CONSULT Consult the Police Surgeon prior to allowing the detainee to take any prescribed medicine

C
CODE
9.6

- SAFEKEEPINGThe custody officer is responsible for safekeeping
- OPPORTUNITY The custody officer must give the detainee the opportunity to take the prescribed medicine at the proper time
- CONTROLLED DRUGS See Medication - Controlled Drugs post
- SERIOUS CONDITION If the detainee has, or claims to need, medication for a heart condition, diabetes, epilepsy or some similar condition, the police surgeon must be consulted (see also Code C 9.2)
- PARACETAMOL May be kept for prisoners (per force instruction or per doctor) and its use recorded. Consider the advantages of using soluble versions to stop prisoners hording this potentially dangerous drug.

General Advice

- Police officer should **never give medication**. Allow the detainee to take some.

- **Never allow** prisoner to take loose tablets. Be aware of suicide attempts. Check medication against any prescription and that the prescription applies to the person.

- Satisfy yourself that they are **necessary** and **recently prescribed**

- If the medication is a **controlled drug,** eg methadone in liquid form, consider having the prescription changed as the liquid may have been adulterated.

- As this is a **high risk area** never let a prisoner take any medication without **checking** with one or more of:

  i   the police surgeon always and

  ii   prisoner's GP or

  iii dispensing chemist.

- Consider the **timing** of medication. Does he need it whilst in custody? Can it be deferred until his own GP or a police surgeon is available?

- If the required medication is not with the prisoner, consider asking a friend/relative/officer to **collect** same.

- Consider the **access** to medication by other custody staff. Do not seal away in his property bag. Best practice is to have a secure cupboard for easier access.

- Generally prisoners are not allowed to **retain medication** but this may be necessary in the case of inhalers or anti-acid tablets.

- If an inhaler etc is **retained delete** against his signature on the **custody record**.

- If medication is **purchased** or **obtained** subsequent to the initial detention, **add** to the **custody record**.

- Consider or seek advice as to whether some **medication** would **prejudice the prisoner** at some future procedure, such as an interview when drowsy from tablets.

  Example of an entry on the custody record regarding **medication**:(it is advisable to use red ink, a 'Medication' stamp, or highlight such entries to stand out for the following shift).

CUSTODY RECORD – MEDICATION
Must   • **Record any medication a detainee has with him on arrival**   • **Record any medication he claims he will need but does not have with him**

Advise to • Record any enquiries made regarding the nature or necessity of the medication.
     • Record if the medication is a controlled drug.
     • The exact dosage required and the interval between doses.
     • Any arrangements made to obtain the medication.
     • Any medication retained by the prisoner against signature.

0900   Has 10 tablets of (full name) on arrival. Confirmed with Police Surgeon Jones required every four hours for allergic reactions. Taken 0800 today. Confirmed prescription and requirement details with Dr Bainbridge (ie 0171 123 1234) the prisoner's own GP with the prisoner's permission. Confirms the tablets will not affect his ability to be interviewed REQUIRES one x tablet every four hours. Commenced 0800 hours today.

MEDICATION – CONTROLLED DRUGS

- Confusion arises between **controlled and prescribed drugs.**

- Many drugs are only available on prescription. Some of these drugs are controlled drugs under Misuse of Drugs Act, but **not all prescribed medicines are controlled drugs**.

- This is an important distinction for the custody officer. **If in doubt a check should be made** with a dispensing chemist, medical practitioner or hospital.

C
CODE
9.5

- **No police officer may administer controlled drugs** subject to the Misuse of Drugs Act 1971 for this purpose. A person may administer such drugs to himself only under the personal supervision of the police surgeon.

- Many forces have a **policy** on the administration and safekeeping of controlled drugs.

- The phrase '**personal supervision**' as used in Code C 9.5, means a personal or telephone consultation with the police surgeon, who may permit self-administration. If in doubt the custody officer should discuss it with police surgeon and if necessary ask him to attend.

C
CODE
9.B

- It is important to bear in mind that illness, drugs or injury (such as to the head) can give symtoms of drunkeness etc and that withdrawal from drugs can be harmful, therefore the surgeon should be called, when in doubt, as quickly as possible.

HANDLING PRISONERS AND REMEDIAL ACTION

Before searching

Obtain information regarding the medical condition, history of violence or complaining about police etc and what risk there is to custody staff, via:

- Speak to prisoner or friends/relatives
- Information systems – PNC/force intelligence
- Observations

Prisoner should help

- Searching
    - i should empty own pocket linings
    - ii wear gloves if necessary for final police search
    - iii document carefully
    - iv avoid confusing descriptions on custody records
- Medical advice/treatment
    - i any open wounds – insist prisoner cleans wound and dresses wound
    - ii get advice from police surgeon regarding treatment for prisoner
    - iii get advice also for protection of custody staff
    - iv consider all custody staff being immunised against hepatitis B if not already force policy

Remedial action

Any leakage of bodily fluids especially blood should be washed well with bleach or other similar substance.

Any blood on hands etc. should be washed with diluted bleach followed by soap and water.

When there is a **known** hepatitis B prisoner and it is suspected his blood has mixed with the officer's (or other person) during a fight by splashing onto a spot on officer's face or cut on hand etc, custody officer should seek immediate medical aid.

An injection to combat hepatitis B can be effective if given shortly after the blood contamination. Force medical officers will normally arrange such an injection.

Urine, vomit etc in cells should be cleaned up as soon as possible. Custody or cleaning staff should be protected. The custody officer should make sure that bleach, other cleaning fluids, mops, buckets, disposable gloves and washable overalls are available.

Communicate with rest of staff and other shifts – place a notice on cells containing verminous, infectious or sick prisoners.

Prisoners with bowel problems should be placed in a cell with a toilet (if available). Minimal contact with such prisoner is advised.

Consider using disposable gloves to serve all meals. This is hygienic for the prisoner and protects the staff.

Ensure custody record is updated regarding such risks and danger to staff.

SECURITY OF PRISONERS

The security of the custody suite and cell block should never be compromised or underestimated. Most forces have suffered the indignity and gross embarrassment of persons escaping from custody. Disciplinary action normally follows with the possibility of criminal charges being brought, ie common law escape.

Common law escape –
Unlimited imprisonment and fine

This offence is committed where a person has been arrested and gains his liberty with the use of force before being delivered up by due course of the law. Besides the person who regains his liberty and any other person who aids the escape, this offence can be committed by **the custodian, who negligently allows the prisoner to escape**.

There is a rebuttable presumption of negligence, therefore the custodian would have to be in a position to prove he wasn't negligent.

RULES OF CUSTODY SUITE

- Cell keys to be kept safely.

- Not given to any persons other than custody office staff.

- Never let other officers lock prisoners in or out of cells.

- Large heavy fob on keys to prevent officers misplacing or taking keys home after duty.

- Don't make it easy for visitors to take copies, ie not to be kept and labelled '**cell keys**' where visitors have access.

- Spare set of keys to be available – officers have been known to lock themselves in a cell whilst in possession of the keys. If the prisoner then becomes violent another set of keys is essential to get the officer out.

- Don't allow any person in the cell block without an escort of custody office staff.

- It is the custody officer's responsibility should anything go wrong!

One case where a solicitor was locked in a cell to interview a violent suspect illustrates the pressures on a custody officer. No one answered the push button emergency call or the solicitor's banging on the steel door. It was only when he called the police station on his mobile telephone that the solicitor was released.

Had the solicitor been injured or killed, the custody officer could well have faced charges and disciplinary action.

Objects in custody suite

Cell corridors, interview/fingerprint rooms, exercise yards, toilets showers, reception and doctor's surgery are all potential battle grounds with violent prisoners.

It should be borne in mind that innocent objects such as typewriters, rulers, chairs, tables have all been used as weapons. When equipping a custody suite thought should be given to preventing objects becoming weapons.

Rubbish or stores should not be allowed to accumulate in these areas.

Only allow inventory objects, not items such as glass milk bottles, stolen bicycles, dustbins, bottles of bleach, etc.

Cells and other areas should be searched before and after use:

- To see whether any interference has taken place with the fabric, furniture or fitting which may assist an escape, cause injury or form the basis of a charge

- To see if any articles have been hidden by the prisoner.

Lock-up Rules

As fate sometimes works it has been known that the instant a prisoner has been taken out of his cell for a morning wash, all the doors to the outside of the police station were open. You have probably seen for yourself on early shift the outside doors of the station propped open as waste paper etc is being loaded into a van, inner doors being propped open by cleaners scrubbing the floors and last but not least, the custody suite door open as breakfast arrives. The perfect opportunity for the agile nineteen-year-old to make a dash for freedom!

Depending on the layout of your station certain doors must be locked before taking prisoners out of their cells.

The use of mirrors or videos could be considered for custody staff to see what is happening around blind corners.

When prisoners are being moved it is the custody officer's responsibility to have sufficient escorts and the appropriate doors locked.

It is normally the custody officer's responsibility to ensure the security of prisoners being moved around the police station, to a doctor/hospital or to court. Only when the prisoner is handed over to another authorised person, is released or is returned to the cells, can the escort be dispensed with. See at the end of this chapter, section 39(2)(a) of PACE regarding transferring his responsibilities to the investigation officer.

Where cells are being used as store-rooms for furniture, bleach and other similar articles, these rooms should be locked before prisoners are moved.

Property given to prisoners by visitors

Many visitors, solicitors, medical staff or even other police officers can leave matches or lighters with a prisoner.

Money and pens or pencils are also given.

Solicitors' mobile telephones and mini tape recording machines also cause problems and your custody suite should have a policy for such items.

Where property is brought in to be given to a prisoner, always transfer to the prisoner via a member of the custody staff. Never let property be given directly to the prisoner.

Explain the rules to visitors etc and thoroughly check all items.

Whether visitors take away or bring property in, always endorse the custody record, together with whether the prisoner was searched before and/or after the visit.

See Chapter 2 for how to escort visitors.

Custody staff should be alert to prisoners passing items of value to visitors, flushing such items down a toilet, dropping or otherwise secreting an object.

COMPLAINTS REGARDING TREATMENT

There are a growing number of complaints against custody officers arising directly from incidents or peripheral to other incidents.

Complaints by or on behalf of a detained person about maltreatment since arrest should be reported as soon as practicable to an inspector or above not connected with the case.

<table>
<tr><td>C
CODE
9.1 & 9.7</td></tr>
</table>

Complaints concerning a possible assault or unnecessary or unreasonable force should also be reported. Again a police surgeon must be called as soon as practicable.

NOTE

Difficulties can arise when prisoners are examined by their own, or a hospital doctor following injury etc. This does not negate the need for an examination by the police surgeon for evidential purposes etc.

The buck stops here and a full record of all actions should be made on the custody record.

CUSTODY RECORD – COMPLAINTS	
Must	• **Record arrangements for examination by a police surgeon** • **Record complaint** • **Record relevant comments from custody officer**

Advise to	• Fully record any complaint
	• Fully record any incident giving rise to a complaint and detainee's demeanour (if relevant)
	• Record the name and details of any person subject of the complaint and his demeanour (if relevant).
	• Record any physical evidence observed or seized.
	• Record inspector to whom complaint recorded.
	• Record any subsequent procedures:
	  i arrangement to seal cell
	  ii to obtain expert assistance
	  iii scenes of crime or forensic arrangements.

No example has been written to illustrate this custody record entry. An example would probably run into pages as the whole incident should be fully recorded.

With reference to the 'custody officer comments' above, he should be aware of making comments not under caution when a crime is alleged.

Responsibilities in relation to persons detained

To reiterate the opening of this chapter -

PACE
S 39(1)

It shall be the duty of the custody officer to ensure that:

(a) All persons in police custody at the station are treated in accordance with this Act and any Code of Practice issued under it and relating to the treatment of persons in police detention

(b) All matters which this Act or Codes of Practice require to be recorded are recorded in the custody records

If the custody officer, transfers or permits the transfer of a prisoner under this Act or Codes to the custody of:

(i) The investigating officer

(ii) An officer having charge of that person outside the police station

then the custody officer's duties under section.39(1)(a) above shall cease.

The duty shall pass to (i) or (ii) above.

When the prisoner is returned to the custody officer by the investigating officer, the investigating officer shall have a duty to report to the custody officer whether this section and the Codes of Practice have been complied with.

CUSTODY RECORD – TRANSFEREES

Advise to
- Record transfer of custody officer's role
- Person to whom duties transferred
- Record of transfer
- Record any advice given, eg exceptional risk/medical condition, escort requirements, or security arrangements.
- Time of transfer
- Any effect on relevant time, eg to hospital
- Time returned to custody suite
- Check that all records comply with the Codes whilst detainee absent.

1000   Transferred into the custody of DS123 A.Galloway for the purpose of searching for evidence near the scene of the crime. Advised me exceptional risk of escape and requested two escorting officers and use of handcuffs outside the police vehicle. Authorised by custody officer PS 456 Harper.

1200   Returned to custody suite by DS Galloway. All Codes of Practice complied with. No complaints. PS 456 Harper.

MEDICAL PRECAUTIONS FOR POLICE OFFICER

As already stated earlier, blood can be a dangerous substance in the custody suite.

Hepatitis B

Injections should be taken by all custody office staff. Blood test every two years should be made to check that protection still exists.

Elastoplast any open cuts, however small, before working with prisoners.

Stress

The custody suite is a highly stressful posting due to the pressures, poor atmosphere, lack of exercise and being surrounded by possibly infectious persons.

Aim for proper meal breaks away from the custody suite with possibly some exercise for good measure. Take care of oneself by having sufficient rest off duty. Watch for tell-tale signs of irritability, eating or drinking too much, not sleeping etc.

Chapter 4
QUESTIONING

The recent release of several convicted persons for alleged mal-practice by the police when evidence gathering is of great concern.

It is the authors' opinion that part of the remedy is to follow religiously the Codes of Practice and PACE. It is considered that any breach of PACE or the Codes will be strictly and literally interpreted. Any breach, however small, at whatever stage of the investigation, could taint the whole case and result in evidence being excluded and an acquittal.

IN ANY PROCEEDINGS

The court may refuse to allow prosecution evidence, if the admission would have such an adverse effect on the fairness of the case that it should not be admitted.

PACE
S 78 (1)

The use of section 78 will be at the magistrates' or judges' discretion. Any breach of PACE or the Codes could result in the discretion being exercised against the prosecution's case.

INTERVIEWS

Definition of an interview

Q   What is an interview under PACE?
   NB This is a vital question as the word 'interview' is used
   both in PACE and the Codes of Practice.

A   The Codes of Practice give guidance to assist an officer to
   determine what constitutes an interview:

C
CODE
11.1A

An interview is questioning someone about suspected
involvement in a crime. The following are not considered to be
'questioning':

C
CODE
10.1

i   Questioning for information. This is not an interview and
   examples would include:
      'What is your name?'
      'Do you own this vehicle?'

ii   Questioning confined to a search. This is not an interview.
   Examples are:

      'Are these crates of whisky yours?'
      'Have you got the key to this set of drawers?'

   Searches would include:
   • A search under section 1 PACE when a constable can
     stop and search a person, vehicle etc.
   • A search under the Misuse of Drugs Act
   • A search under sections 17, 18, and 32 PACE for
     persons or evidence.

iii   Procedures under section 7 of the Road Traffic Act 1988
   (ie drink driving, specimens and venue) do not constitute
   interviewing for the purpose of this Code.

iv   Questioning regarding a statutory requirement. This is not an interview, despite the fact that he has been CAUTIONED. An example being:

'You have been charged. Are you still refusing your name and address? I must tell you that without your name and address you cannot be given bail and will be detained until the next court.'

C
CODE
10.5C

Other such statutory requirements might include procedures under the 1988 Road Traffic Act.

v   Questioning to verify a written record of any unsolicited comment made by the suspect. An example being:

'You have witnessed PC ADAMS write down a comment you made on arrival at the custody suite. I am giving you the pportunity to read and sign it etc, etc....'

C
CODE
11.13

TRANSFER OF RESPONSIBILITY OF COMPLIANCE WITH CODE DURING INTERVIEW

Q   Who has the responsibility for ensuring that the Codes of Practice have been complied with in interview?
A   The custody officer retains the overall responsibility for determining if a detained person may be delivered into the custody of the interviewing officer.

C
CODE
12.1

However once he has done so the responsibility for complying directly with the Codes of Practice passes over to the interviewing officer. The custody officer must follow certain requirements before and after the interview.

PACE
S 39

CUSTODY RECORD – TRANSFER OF RESPONSIBILITY

Must   Record times the detained person was not in the custody of the custody officer.
Record the reason why he was not in his custody, or any refusal to deliver him into someone else's custody.

1000 hours	DS Ken Smith, officer in case was handed prisoner for interview regarding his suspected involvement in a crime.
1130 hours	Prisoner returned to my custody by DS Ken Smith after interview.

C
CODE
12.9

CAUTIONING

Responsibility to caution

Q   What is the custody officer's responsibility in relation to the cautioning of persons?

A   Generally he has no direct responsibility to caution in his capacity as a custody officer, except through his intial action, when he gives a new prisoner a 'notice of rights' containing the caution.

But he should take an interest in the offence after substantiating any arrest and safeguarding evidence. He should be ready to advise inexperienced officers regarding cautioning.

1   Interviews of arrested persons prior to arrival at the police station (or other authorised place of detention).

C
CODE
11.1

Following an arrest he must not be interviewed except at a police station unless the consequent delay would be likely to:

    (a) Interfere with or harm evidence or person

    (b) Alert other person suspected of offence

    (c) Hinder recovery of property obtained from an offence.

All interviewing in these circumstances should stop once the risk has ended or the questions have been put in order to attempt to end the risk.

NB Questioning – special restrictions

If a person has been arrested by one police force on another's behalf and the period of detention for that offence has not yet begun in accordance with section 41 of the Police and Criminal Evidence Act 1984 questions may not be put to him while in transit between forces except in order to clarify any voluntary statement made by him.

> C
> CODE
> 11.2

> C
> CODE
> 14.1

A police detainee at a hospital may not be questioned without the consent of a responsible doctor.

> C
> CODE
> 14.2 note 14A

If questioning takes place at a hospital, or on the way to or from a hospital, the period concerned counts towards the total period of detention permitted.

Where there is a delay in taking an arrested person to a police station the reasons shall be recorded, when he arrives at a police station.

> PACE
> S 30 (II)

CUSTODY RECORD – INTERVIEWS PRIOR TO ARRIVING AT POLICE STATION

Advise to

    Record place of interview

    Record times commenced and concluded

    Record reasons for the interview and

    Codes of Practice complied with

2315 hours Interviewed in police car when driving from the town centre to try to locate about £1,000,000 worth of antiques, thought to be about to be shipped abroad. Interview concluded at 2330 hours. All Codes of Practice complied with. Information gleaned given to waiting detective by VHF radio.

2 Interviews at a police station

Custody officer and interviews

Q What is the custody officer's prime responsibility in relation to interviews?

A If a police officer wishes to interview, or conduct inquiries requiring the presence of the prisoner, he is responsible for deciding whether to allow it.

> C CODE 12.1

3 Interview prohibitions

Q When may a person not be interviewed or continue to be interviewed?

A1 When he is medically unfit for interview.

In instances in which the custody officer has determined a person in detention requires hospital treatment, or the services of his doctor or a police surgeon, he shall not be interviewed unless found medically fit for interview.

> C CODE note 12B

A2 When he is unfit through drink or drugs.

No person unfit through drink or drugs, when he cannot appreciate the significance of questions and answers, may be questioned. (Except under Annex C for urgent interviews - see later this chapter). Again the police surgeon must be consulted.

> C CODE 12.3

NOTE

A detained person may only be given intoxicating liquor on medical directions. A record must be made of any supplied. It is also advisable to record the medical directions and the medical practitioner concerned.

> C CODE 12.3 & 12.10

A3 Without rest.

In any period of 24 hours a detained person must be allowed at least a continuous 8 hours rest free from:

- Questioning
- Travel
- Other interruptions concerning investigation:
  - i This period should normally be at night
  - ii Delay or interruption only when reasonable grounds to believe would:
    - Involve risk of harm to persons or loss/damage to property
    - Delay unnecessarily person's release from custody

> C CODE 12.2

– Otherwise prejudice outcome of investigation.

iii At the request of the suspect, the appropriate adult or his legal representative.

NOTE

Other allowable interuptions include action under Code C 8 (conditions of detention) or action according to medical advice.

PHYSICAL TREATMENT OF DETAINED PERSON IN INTERVIEW

Q What provisions must be made by the custody officer for the detained person's physical needs during an interview?

A1 As far as practicable interviews shall take place in interview rooms which must be adequately heated, lit and ventilated.

C
CODE
12.4

A2 Persons being questioned or making statements shall not be required to stand.

C
CODE
12.5

A3 Interview breaks shall be at recognised meal times. Short breaks at intervals of approximately two hours subject to the interviewing officer's discretion to delay if reasonable grounds for believing risk of harm to persons or serious loss/damage to property or would delay unnecessarily the person's release from custody or otherwise prejudice the outcome of the investigation.

C
CODE
12.7

NOTE ONE

C
CODE
12.11

Any decision to delay a break and the reasons for it must be recorded.

NOTE TWO

C
CODE
12 C

- Meal breaks should be 45 minutes.

- Short breaks should be 15 minutes.

- Where the interviews are extended or shortened to facilitate release, the breaks can be adjusted.

Good custody officers aware of these needs exercise their power to allow interviews to take place in such a way as to balance welfare against investigation, eg delay long interview until after a recognised meal break.

RIGHTS AND ENTITLEMENTS IN INTERVIEWS

Q   What rights and entitlements is the detained person due, in relation to interviews?

A1 He may be entitled to free, independent legal advice.

A2 He may be entitled to have an appropriate adult present.

A3 He may be entitled to have an interpreter.

LEGAL ADVICE AND INTERVIEW

Q Can a person who wants legal advice be interviewed or continue to be interviewed without it?

A1 Before an interview or on recommencement of an interview the interviewing officer should remind the suspect of his entitlement to free legal advice and the reminder recorded as part of the interview.

C
CODE
11.1A &
11.1

NOTE

The reminder given by the interviewer is similar to the legal formula given by the custody officer when the detainee first arrives.

It may be advisable for the custody officer to include an entry in the custody record formally recording compliance with the legal formula provision prior to starting the interview.

A2 A person who wants legal advice may not be interviewed or continue to be interviewed until the legal advice has been given unless there are special circumstances.

C
CODE
6.6 & annex B

Special Circumstances

There are special circumstances and the interview is authorised by a superintendent who has reasonable grounds for believing that:

EITHER his detention is connected with a serious arrestable offence and:

    i will lead to interference with or harm to evidence of a serious arrestable offence or interference with or physical harm to others; or

    ii will lead to alerting others suspected of committing such an offence or

    iii will hinder the recovery of property obtained in pursuance of such an offence.

Where the serious arrestable offence is either a drugs trafficking offence or one covered by confiscation orders, these are also exceptions.

OR Delay

<table>
<tr><td>C
CODE
6.6(b)</td><td></td></tr>
</table>

    i   delay will involve immediate risk of harm to persons or serious loss of or damage to property; or

    ii where a solicitor has agreed to attend, awaiting his arrival would cause unreasonable delay to the investigation.

NOTE ONE

C CODE 6.7

Where (i) above applies, once sufficient information to end the risk has been obtained, questioning must stop until legal advice is given.

In considering if (ii) above applies, the officer should ask the solicitor to estimate his arrival time. The officer should then take into account:

C CODE note 6A

- the period detention is permitted,
- the time of day, ie period of rest,
- the requirements of other investigations.

Where the interview is to go ahead without the solicitor, the solicitor should be informed how long the interview could wait to give him an opportunity to provide alternative legal advice.

NOTE TWO

When a detainee is allowed a solicitor, he cannot be interviewed without the solicitor, if:

C CODE 6.8

- Present at the station
- On his way
- Easily telephoned

122

OR Solicitor Unavailable

UNLESS a solicitor cannot be present at the interview and the interview is authorised by an Inspector.

A solicitor selected by the detained person or nominated or chosen from a list:

> C
> CODE
> 6.6(C)

    i   cannot be contacted

    ii has indicated he does not wish to be contacted

    iii having been contacted has declined to attend; **and**

the person has been offered the 'Duty Solicitor Scheme, (if in operation) but has declined or a duty solicitor is unavailable.

OR Change of Mind

When a person requests legal advice but later changes his mind, before or during interview and has agreed in writing or on tape to be interviewed, an inspector must sanction the interview to start or re-commence. Usually this exchange takes place outside the interview and the custody record is used to record the events, the reasons for change of mind and the inspector's authorisation. All of which must be confirmed again, belt and braces style, at the beginning of the record of interview.

NOTE ONE

Such an authorisation can be given over the telephone.

> C
> CODE
> 6.1

NOTE TWO

Unless Annex B (Special Circumstances ante) apply, the detainee must be told of a solicitor's arrival and given the opportunity to see him, even if this means interrupting an interview.

> C
> CODE
> 6.13

NOTE THREE

A person who requests legal advice should have the opportunity to consult:

> C
> CODE
> note 6B

- his own solicitor; or
- one from that firm, or
- a duty solicitor (where in operation); or

- one from a list; or
- up to two alternatives.

If these attempts are unsuccessful the custody officer has discretion to allow further attempts **unless** the detainee changes his mind **and** gives his agreement (in writing or on tape) **and** an inspector gives his agreement

Solicitor defined (See under 'Stopping or delaying rights' in chapter two)

Conflict of interest

C
CODE
note 6G

Subject to Annex B of Code C (ante) a solicitor can advise more than one client in an investigation. It is up to the solicitor's professional code of conduct. If any delay, Code 6.6(b) above, could apply.

Misconduct

C
CODE
6.9 6.10 & 6.11

Interviewing officers may require solicitors or their trainees, non-accredited or probationary representatives presumed to be guilty of misconduct to leave the interview and consult a superintendent or above (if not readily available, an inspector or above) as to whether the solicitor should be allowed to return to the interview and/or whether to report to the Law Society.

NOTE

Note 6D of Code C gives excellent advice concerning what is and is not acceptable conduct.

The custody officer may become involved in this process by arranging for alternative legal advice and generally advising, superintendents, inspectors and investigating officers

---

CUSTODY RECORD – RECORD OF LEGAL ACCESS

Must Record any request for legal advice.
Record any action to secure legal advice.
Record any interview begun in the absence of legal advice following a request, the reason why, and the authorising officer.
Record any decision to request a solicitor etc to leave an interview, the reason why and officer concerned.
Record any attendance of a solicitor and the prisoner's decision to see or not to see the solicitor.
Where a non-accredited or probationary representative is refused access to the police station record, when their employer contacted and the fact that he was given an opportunity to make alternative arrangements.
Record any change of mind by the detained person in relation to legal advice and any agreement by an inspector or above.

A typical entry, but not covering all the above points.

0900   Request for legal advice by prisoner from his solicitor, Mr S Smyth.

0905   Contacted Mr S Smyth ETA 0930 hours.

0930   Mr S Smyth arrived.

0935   Prisoner refused to see Mr Smyth saying 'All solicitors are rubbish. I just wanted to see his face'.

0940   Mr Smyth left station, prisoner declined any legal advice (obtain prisoner's signature or show refusal).

APPROPRIATE ADULT

Q When must an appropriate adult be present at interview?
AND
What advice must the custody officer give the adult?

C
CODE
11.14

A1 He must be present at the interview of:

- a juvenile
- a person who has a mental disorder
- a person who is mentally disturbed

NOTE

The usual exceptions of 'unless interfering with or harm to evidence or people, alerting others or hindering recovery of property' apply under Code C 11.1 and Annex C

See also Chapter 7 on Special Groups

C
CODE
11.16

A2 The adult should be informed:

- that he is not simply an observer
- that he is there to advise the prisoner
- he should observe whether the interview is proper and fair, and
- he should assist communication with the prisoner.

CUSTODY RECORD – ATTENDANCE OF APPROPRIATE ADULT

Advise to record

- Any decision to secure the attendance of an appropriate adult

- The reasons for that decision

- Any arrangements made for their attendance

- Full details of the appropriate adult including the relationship to the detained person

- Any note of rights and entitlements given in the presence of the appropriate adult or repeated upon his subsequent arrival

- Any decision taken by the appropriate adult in respect of them

- The appropriate adult's presence and/or agreement to any procedure undertaken in relation to the detained person

2047	Parents of 12-year-old boy called. They had no transport or suitable buses and stated not enough money for a taxi. A police car was sent.
2057	Mother of detainee arrived, a Mrs Tracy Small. I explained her son had declined legal advice and Mrs Small agreed (signature).

INFERENCES FROM SILENCE

Investigating officers grappling with 'Significant Statements or Silence' and 'Special Warnings' will seek advice from custody officer, despite the fact that it is not a part of their role. Custody officers may feel a need to familiarise themselves with the appropriate areas of Code C namely 10.5A to 10.5C and 11.2A.

INTERPRETERS

Q1 What persons need an interpreter?
        and

Q2 When must the interpreter be present?

A1 Suitably qualified interpreters are required for detained
persons:
* Who are deaf or speech handicapped. C Code 13.5
* Who have difficulty understanding English. C Code 13.2
* Where the appropriate adult acting for a juvenile appears
  deaf or there is doubt about his hearing or speaking
  ability. C Code 13.6

A2 The interpreter must be present unless Code C 11.1 or Code C
Annex C (urgent interviews) applies,
and

C
CODE
13.5 & 13.6

In relation to the deaf and speech handicapped unless:
* The impaired person agrees in writing.
* The appropriate adult agrees in writing.

INTERPRETING LEGAL ADVICE AND POLICE INTERPRETERS

*Q1 What action do I take if the prisoner cannot communicate
with the solicitor?*

Q2 When can a police officer act as interpreter?

A1 Whether because of language, hearing or speech difficulties,
an interpreter must be called.

C
CODE
13.9

A2 A police officer cannot interpret for a prisoner who is
receiving legal advice.
In all other cases a police officer can interpret if:
* The prisoner (or appropriate adult) agrees in writing; or
* The interview is tape recorded in accordance with the
  Code of Practice.

PERSONS CHARGED AND INTERPRETER

C
CODE
13.10

Where the person is charged and there is doubt about hearing,
speaking ability, understanding English and the custody officer
cannot effectively communicate, then an interpreter must be
called as soon as practicable to explain the offence and any other
information from the custody officer.

INTERPRETERS ARE FREE OF CHARGE

The detained person should be informed that interpreters will be provided at the public expense.

C
CODE
13.8

LANGUAGE LINE

Custody officer should be aware of LANGUAGE LINE which is a telephone interpreting service providing 140 languages 24 hours a day.

Connection to a trained interpreter from ANY telephone takes about one minute. It is used by custody officers in establishing prisoners' personal details, any medical problems and reading 'rights and entitlements' to them. In drink/driving cases it is advised that a supervisory officer be consulted as Language Line should not normally be used for evidential purposes or statement taking.

A three way conferencing facility is possible should custody Officers wish to speak to non-English speaking members of the detained person's family etc.

Officers whose force is under contract to Language Line should quote their force code and collar number.

Forces not under contract can have ad hoc access with the approval of a named supervisory officers who must agree to meet the quoted charges.

Interpreters (24 hours) 0181 983 2800 and administration 0181 983 4042

NOTE

Local authority social services departments usually keep lists of interpreters for the deaf. The Community Relations Council usually keep lists for those not understanding English.

CUSTODY RECORD – RECORD OF INTERPRETERS

Must record

Any action to call an interpreter

Any agreement to be interviewed in the absence of an interpreter

Advise to record

Any offer of the provision of an interpreter at public expense

The presence of or notification to the interpreter in relation to any procedures taken as a result of a request by the detained person

2348 hrs	Interpreter Ahmed Akbar called for prisoner who only speaks Urdu.
0005 hrs	Mr Akbar arrived and informed that the prisoner had been in contact with his consular official, who was going to visit the prisoner as soon as possible.
0010 hrs	Prisoner informed that the interpreter fees were at the public's expense.

TAPE RECORDED INTERVIEWS

Tape recorded interviews are conducted in accordance with Code of Practice E on tape recording under the terms of section 60 PACE.

The custody officer is given certain specific responsibilities under the Code which are detailed as follows:

Interviews not requiring tape recording

Q   Under what circumstances can interviews be conducted other than by tape recording?

A   The decision not to tape the interview has been authorised by the custody officer because either:

> E
> CODE
> 3.3

   i   It is not practicable due to equipment failure or interview rooms not being available

   ii   It is clear that there will be no prosecution.

NOTE ONE

The custody officer shall record his reasons, given that it could be the subject of judicial review.

> E
> CODE
> note 3K

In practice custody officer will have to prioritise the tape recording of serious offences. Queuing is often neccessary, given the urgency imposed by relevant time.

> E
> CODE
> note 3J

Complaints

Q   What is the custody officer's involvement subsequent to any complaint by or on behalf of the person being questioned?

A   In all cases the custody officer must be informed of the nature and existence of the complaint.

> E
> CODE
> 4.6
> note 4H

131

C
CODE
9 & 12.8

If the complaint refers to anything in Code C or Code E the custody officer shall be called immediately and wherever possible speak to the person being interviewed while the tape recorder is still running. The interview may then continue or be terminated at the discretion of the interviewing officer.

E
CODE
note 4J

If the complaint is about another matter, the interviewing officer may inform the custody officer at the conclusion of the interview, having first informed the complainant of his intention to do so.

NOTE ONE

C
CODE
9.1

The custody officer should make a report of the complaint to an inspector or above as soon as practicable. If the complaint is one of assault or the unreasonable use of force then a police surgeon must be called as soon as practicable.

NOTE TWO

Smoking can be a problem in interview and may be a matter of force policy. It is advised that where no guidance is given, smoking can be allowed if all parties present consent, especially as it avoids allegations of oppression by the detainee. However where the detainee does not wish to smoke there should be no smoking.

COMPLIANCE WITH CODE OF PRACTICE

PACE
S 39

Where the custody officer transfers the prisoner into the custody of the interviewing officer, it is advisable that he reminds the officer that he has taken over responsibility for compliance with the Codes of Practice.

Similarly it may be necessary to remind the interviewing officer of his duty to report to the custody officer of the manner of his compliance and record the fact of compliance in the custody record.

TAPES AND EQUIPMENT

*Q What is expected
of the custody officer
regarding tapes
and equipment?*

A1 In many forces the custody officer is responsible for issuing and
receiving interview tapes, as well as for their ultimate security.
It is advisable to ensure adequate supplies of tapes and forms
are available at the start of duty. You may also consider the
practice of recording the issue of master tapes by referencing
the custody record with the unique reference number.

A2 Similarly the custody officer is generally presumed to be the
expert when things go wrong with the equipment. You should
familiarise yourself with it. More importantly you should
have a working knowledge of the procedures detailed in the
Codes in relation to broken tapes and the like.

A3 On occasions problems arise with the labelling of used tapes,
the security of and the access of them, eg if the tape is
labelled on the wrong side, when played back it appears
blank. Many a detective has a panic attack at this stage, but
when the experienced custody officer comes to the rescue and
merely turns over and rewinds the tape, all is well.

Local force procedure and PACE guidance should be fully
understood regarding access to tapes at a later date, the
central tape library system and the problems that arise daily
with tapes.(See HO Circular 13/95)

E
CODE
4.16

RECORDS OF TAPE RECORDING

The majority of ancillary records in relation to tape recorded
interviews are recorded on specialised stationery or in the
interviewing officer's official note book.

However there are some matters which must be recorded on the
custody record.

CUSTODY RECORD – TAPE RECORDED INTERVIEWS

Must   Record the authority not to tape record the interview and a note of the specific terms of the reasons.

Record complaints by or on behalf of the interviewee, the person to whom they were made and any action taken by him or any officers subsequently

Advise to record

A note of the master tape reference number

An entry testifying that the codes of practice were complied with throughout the interview.

Plus all the other requirements of interviews generally.

1810 hrs - Master tape 8/123/92 issued to DS Dalrymple for the interview of the prisoner.

2000 hrs - DS Dalrymple states that interview concluded and that all Codes of Practice were complied with throughout the interview.

URGENT INTERVIEWS

Q   *When may a custody officer allow a vulnerable person to be interviewed as a matter of urgency without the appropriate safeguards?*

C
CODE
Annex C

A   When authorised by a superintendent or above who considers delay likely to:

C
CODE
11.1

- Interfere/harm
- Evidence or people
- Alert other suspects
- Hinder recovery of property

The following persons may be interviewed:

- Heavily under influence of drink or drugs
- Juvenile or mentally handicapped or disordered person without appropriate adult
- Difficulty in understanding English or hearing difficulty without an interpreter

Also see Chapter 7 on Special Groups.

NOTE

When sufficient information has been obtained questioning must cease.

CUSTODY RECORD – URGENT INTERVIEWS

Must Record the grounds for any such interview

Advise to record

The type of person to be interviewed ie drunk, juvenile, hearing difficulty etc

The specific nature of the risk, ie harm to persons, loss of property.

Name and rank of authorising officer

Signature of authorising officer or method of obtaining authorisation, eg by telephone

---

1515 hrs Prisoner interviewed whilst drunk as believed to have left 5-year-old daughter somewhere by herself. Concern for well-being of daughter.

Superintendent R Lowery authorised the interview.

R Lowery – Superintendent

CHECK LIST FOR PRE-INTERVIEW FOR THE CUSTODY OFFFICER

Prior to the commencement of an interview at a police station of a person detained, it is advisable to ensure that a number of procedures essential to safeguarding the evidence have been complied with. These are the responsibility of the custody officer and must be adequately documented.

(a) Have any interviews been conducted prior to this interview?
(b) Is the person fit for interview?
- Medically fit
- Unfit through drink or drugs
- Adequate period of rest
- Adequate meal break

135

(c) Has the person been offered free independent legal advice?

(d) Were the person's decisions and any subsequent action recorded?
- Any decision to deny the person access to legal advice
- Where a solicitor is not available – the facilities offered and the number of attempts to contact a solicitor.

(e) Has the detained person changed his mind?

(f) Has any non-accredited or probationary representative been denied access?
- The offer to make alternative arrangements
- What action taken
- Name and rank of authorising officer ie superintendent or inspector.

(g) Has any communication or private consultation with a solicitor taken place prior to interview?

(h) Is the detained person a citizen of an independent Commonwealth country or a foreign national?
- Any provisions offered or actioned in relation to this *(See Chapter 7 on Special Groups)*

(i) Does the prisoner require an appropriate adult?
- The specific adult contacted
- Reasons for choice of appropriate adult, ie parent not available, prior admissions of guilt
- Arrangements made for attendance
- Information offered to the appropriate adult and his decisions ie:
    - Free legal advice
    - His role in the interview
    - Interpreter at public expense
    - Any communication or private consultation with the appropriate adult prior to interview.

(j) Does the prisoner, the custody officer, or an appropriate adult require an interpreter?
- Reason for the requirement
- Hearing, speaking disability/fail to understand English
- Arrangements made to obtain an interpreter
- Name and status of the interpreter, eg specialist social services or police officer.
- The information subject to the interpreter, eg information supplied under the Codes of Practice.

(k) Was the interview an urgent interview under Code C Annex C?
(See also Code C 11.1)
- Which immediate risk involved?
- The authorising officer
- Reason for prisoner's vulnerability?

(l) How was the interview recorded, ie tape or otherwise, and
any objections or decisions in this area
- The decision regarding the method of recording and the
reasons, ie tape
- Contemporaneous notes
- Retrospective notes
- Any objections to the recording
- The prisoner's decision in relation to the record
- Reasons for the choice of recording method
- Any consultation in relation to the above, eg solicitor or
investigating officer.

(m) The details of the interview
- The place of interview
- All the persons present and their status, eg police officer,
solicitor, appropriate adult, observer
- The time of commencement of the interview.

(n) Special provisions for the interview in relation to care and
custody
- Security arrangements, eg handcuffs
- Treatment of detained person, eg drinks provided.

UNSOLICITED COMMENTS AND INFORMAL INTERVIEWS

Custody staff are often in a unique position to receive
spontaneous admissions from detained persons.

Similarly they can prevent officers from compromising future
interview evidence by seeking to influence or elicit admission
through a 'general chat'.

The custody staff can assist them to safeguard evidence obtained
in good faith, or prevent evidence being tainted by association
with legitimate discussions 'off tape'.

The above can be achieved simply by preventing dubious
practices, giving good advice or ensuring the proper recording of
such admissions.

UNSOLICITED COMMENTS

Q How can unsolicited comments made by a detained person outside the interview be dealt with under the Codes of Practice?

C
CODE
11.13

A1 A written record should be made of any unsolicited comments made outside the interview.

The record should be timed and signed by the maker.

Where practicable the prisoner should be given the opportunity to read the record.

C
CODE
11.D

He should sign it as correct using the formula of words contained in the Codes of Practice, or indicate areas he considers inaccurate.

Any refusal to sign should be recorded.

NOTE

This could include comments made in response to being informed of the reason for arrest or detention, or on being asked why he declined legal advice.

A2 However, officers should be aware of the need to act fairly in the face of these admissions or of an indication that such an admission is about to be made.

A decided case may help to illustrate the situation:

In R v Woodall & Ors [1989] Crim LR 288 a defendant volunteered information after being interviewed and charged. During a welfare visit he started by saying 'this is off the record'. The court found that such volunteered information should be excluded under section 78 PACE, ie taking into account all the circumstances of the case the adverse effect on the fairness of the proceedings was such that the court ought not to admit it.

To allow it would amount to allowing evidence obtained by a 'trick'. Presumably the 'trick' resulted from not telling the defendant that there was no such thing as 'off the record', and by not cautioning him under Code C 10.

INFORMAL INTERVIEWS

Q   What are the evidential implications of allowing officers the opportunity of a 'general chat' prior to interview?
A   Any conversation which a police officer has with a detained person prior to interview will be open to allegations of misconduct. This is particularly so if admissions are made in a subsequent interview.

A custody officer must satisfy himself of the necessity for such an exchange and should advise an officer contemplating this course of action of the possible consequences. It may be advisable that any such 'welfare visit' should be undertaken by the custody staff.

CASE LAW

Some case law can add more meaning to the above.

In R v Sparks [1991] Crim LR 128 an informal and friendly conversation in the defendant's house before his eventual arrest was found by the court to amount to an interview.

The Codes of Practice should have been followed.

If in doubt the Codes should always be followed. As has been seen in several recent cases, failure to observe the Codes in similar situations has resulted in the evidence being excluded.

RIGHTING WRONGS

On occasions the custody officer's questioning of officers regarding compliance with the Codes of Practice whilst a detainee is out of his custody provokes disclosures about possible breaches.

His advice may facilitate proper remedial action, such as photo-copying written notes of interview and serving them on the defence, the detained person not having had a chance to review the notes previously.

At the very least officers can be advised to bring any possible breaches of the codes to the attention of a Crown Prosecution Service official and prevent a later embarrassment by the defence.

CHECK LIST FOR POST INTERVIEW FOR THE CUSTODY OFFICER

Upon the conclusion of an interview at a police station of a person detained, it is advisable to ensure that the procedures for which the custody officer is directly responsible have been complied with.

Those which the interviewing officer is responsible for should be checked likewise.

Both procedures should have been adequately documented.

(a) The time the interview was completed.

(b) The time the detained person was returned into the custody of the custody officer.

(c) Any discrepancy between these times and the reason for it.

(d) A report from the interviewing officer to the effect that the Codes of Practice have been complied with.

(e) Any actual or perceived failure to strictly observe the requirements of the Codes of Practice and any remedial action taken.

(f) Any complaints made during the interview and any action taken in response.

(g) Any request made by the detained person or any other person present in the interview and any action taken to comply with them.

(h) Any breaks in the interview or the provision of refreshments etc.

(i) Any changes to the persons present during the interview and the reason for them, ie solicitor required to leave the interview for disruption.

(j) Any equipment failure and remedial action in relation to it.

(k) Any information or procedure held in abeyance pending the completion of the interview, eg reviews of detention or meals.

(l) Any requests made by or on behalf of the detained person upon leaving the interview.

Chapter 5
REVIEWS

This chapter deals with time, in particular with the timing of detention reviews and problems related to relevant time.

Many people seem to assume wrongly that there is only **one** starting point for the two essential PACE Act clocks. Indeed some people appear to mistakenly treat the two concepts of review time and relevant time as one. A detainee transferred from elsewhere may have been reviewed a number of times before the relevant time begins for the offence for which he is under arrest.

Review timing is the simplest of the two concepts. It has only one start time, ie the moment detention was first authorised with regular periods of time within which reviews must be undertaken. Once started it only stops when the detainee leaves police detention.

Relevant time is a much more complex subject. It has five possible start times.

It can be stopped when the detainee is:

- In the custody of a court
- At hospital, or
- Bailed (only to restart when he returns). In general terms it:
  - runs out at the end of 24 hours
  - may be extended to 36 hours by a superintendent
  - may be extendedto up to 96 hours by a court.

Relevent Time Starts
General

1 Time of arrival at 1st police station

2 Person attending voluntarily and subsequently arrested:

Time of arrest

3 Person arrested outside England and Wales:

Earliest time between

i Time of arrival at 1st police station in police force on whose behalf he was arrested or

ii 24 hours after entering England or Wales

4 Person arrested but not questioned by force two on behalf of force one

Earliest time between

i Time of arrival at 1st police station in force one, or

ii 24 hours after his arrest

5 Person is arrested for an offence and detained in force one. Arrest is sought in force two for 'another' offence. The detainee is transferred to force two without being questioned about the 'other' offence:

Earliest time between

i Time of arrival at the first police station in force two, or

ii 24 hours from the time he left the place where he was detained in force one

Temporary stoppage only for:

- In custody of a court
- At a hospital, or en route to or from a hospital (if not questioned)
- On police bail to a police station

REVIEWS OF POLICE DETENTION

Q *What is meant by 'police detention?'*
A Police detention is defined in section 118(2) and includes:

persons taken to the police station after arrest;
persons arrested at the police station after attending there voluntarily, or accompanying a constable there and detained there or elsewhere, eg at hospital, assisting officers' enquiries outside the station etc but not including detention at court after charge.

Q *Who may act as a review officer?*
A The type of review officer is dependent upon whether the prisoner has been charged:

PACE
S 40(1)

- The custody officer where prisoner has been arrested and charged
- An inspector or above not directly involved in the investigation where arrested but not charged.

NOTE ONE

Prisoners remanded into custody for enquiries into other offences are mentioned in R v Sale and Vittori (1990) Luton Crown Court, February 14 1990. It was held that a remand prisoner who has not been charged shall be reviewed by an inspector or above.

The rationale for this decision is simply that the prisoner had not been charged with the offence for which he is being detained.

NOTE TWO

A sergeant shall be treated as an inspector when properly authorised to act as an inspector.

PACE
S107(2)

THE TIMING OF REVIEWS

Q   When shall reviews be completed?

A   The starting point for calculating the timing of reviews of detention is the time when detention was first authorised.

Subsequent timings are calculated from the time of any previous reviews. The timing of each review must be within the times specified in PACE:

First review
Not later than six hours
after detention first authorised

PACE
S 40(3)

Second review
Not later than nine hours after
the first review.

Subsequent reviews
At intervals of not more than
nine hours.

Informal continuous reviews
The custody officer undertakes these throughout the period of detention.

Postponed reviews

Q Can a review be postponed?

A A review may be postponed when not practicable to carry one out:

PACE
S 40(4)
(5) & (6)

- No review officer readily available
- If being questioned and review officer satisfied that interruption would prejudice the investigation
- If postponed the review should be carried out as soon as practicable
- If reviewed after a postponement this will not affect the time at which any subsequent review is to be carried out.

NOTE: POSTPONED REVIEW

When a review has been postponed for any period of time any subsequent review will not be carried out 9 hours after the last review, but shall be carried out within a period of 9 hours less the period of the postponement.

EXAMPLE

2nd review 2 hours late ie due 10.00 hours and carried out at 12.00 hours.

3rd (or subsequent review) is 2 hours early at 1900 hours. ie 9 hours after 12.00 hours is 2100 hours, minus the 2 hour postponement, makes the 3rd review time as 1900 hours.

Premature reviews

Q Can a review be carried out prematurely?

A The review may be carried out within the specified time. Hence any number of reviews can be undertaken within the time the prisoner is in police detention.

Detainee asleep

The Code of Practice advises that a review be carried out prematurely when a detainee is likely to be asleep.

C
CODE
note 15A

NOTE ONE: PREMATURE REVIEWS

When a review is carried out within the specified period, the next review must be carried out within 9 hours of the premature review.

EXAMPLE

Second review 2 hours early ie 1000hrs instead of 1200 hours.

Third (or subsequent review) should be at the new time ie 1900 hours, not 2100 hours.

NOTE TWO

In some police stations all the review times are harmonised where practicable. This entails all the reviews being undertaken at set times with one full review per shift or relief, ie 0700, 1500, and 2200 hours. Obviously newly arrested persons may represent wild cards in this orderly system, but it does simplify procedures and ensure continuity. (NB This system also allows prisoners a full 8 hours for sleep).

Grounds for continued detention

PACE
S 40(8)
& (10)

Q What are the criteria used by the review officers as grounds for authorising the detainee's continued detention?

A The criteria, like the rank of the review officer, depend upon whether the detainee has been charged.

They largely approximate to the grounds contained in section 37 (prisoner not charged) and section 38 (prisoner charged), being based upon the necessity principle:

BEFORE CHARGE REVIEW (SECTION 37)

1 Must decide whether sufficient evidence to charge or detain him until such a decision can be made

2 If decided insufficient evidence to charge, then release, unless continued detention **necessary** to secure or preserve evidence of offence arrested for

3 Where reasonable grounds for believing (2 above), detention may be authorised

4 Where detention is so authorised, a written record of the grounds of detention to be made as soon as practicable

5 The written record to be made in presence of detainee, who at that time shall be told of reasons for detention.

Condition 5 above does not apply where:

- Incapable of understanding
- Violent or likely to be violent
- In urgent need of medical care

AFTER CHARGE REVIEW (SECTION 38 AS AMENDED)

Once a person has been charged the custody officer must decide whether to detain the suspect. The vast majority of persons will be bailed with or without conditions. For those not granted bail the custody officer must have **reasonable grounds for believing** one or more of the following criteria apply. (Where it is decided to detain, these criteria would apply to subsequent reviews)

To help the reader through this rather complex area we have categorised the criteria into ADULT and JUVENILE-IMPRISONABLE and NON-IMPRISONABLE giving examples where necessary.

1. ADULT

The custody officer should order release from detention **unless** he reasonably believes that:

- name and address not known or in doubt
- the suspect would fail to answer bail at court
- he will interfere with justice or the investigation
- necessary for suspect's own protection, eg the offence is one which disgusts the public at large and he has received several threats or he is suicidal.
- charged with murder, attempted myrder, manslaughter rape or attempted rape and previously convicted of such an offence (or imprisoned if convicted of manslaughter). Section 25 Criminal Justice and Public Order Act 1994.
- defendant is accused of committing (indictable or either way) offence while already on bail. Part I, Sched 1, Bail Act 1976 – 'defendant need not be granted bail'.

(The above criteria apply to both imprisonable and non-imprisonable offences).

The custody officer must now distinguish between imprisonable and non-imprisonable offences:

Imprisonable

- Custody officer has reasonable belief that detention necessary to **prevent** him from committing **an offence**, eg known drug addict charged with 'shoplifting' and custody officer has reasonable grounds to believe he would continue shoplifting regularly to feed his addiction. The reasonable grounds being his admission of living by means of shoplifting and previous offending history (to be recorded on custody record).

Non-Imprisonable

- Custody officer has reasonable belief that detention necessary to prevent harm to other person or to property, eg suspect charged with section 5 Public Order Act 1986, causing harassment, alarm or distress to a neighbour and the custody officer has reasonable grounds to believe he will return to the scene and cause damage or injure the victim.

The reasonable grounds being his threat to throw a brick through the window at the victim (to be entered on the custody record).

NOTE

It is expected that the majority of persons detained will have been charged with imprisonable offences. Only rarely will the more limited criteria under 'non-imprisonable offences' be required to detain the suspect after charge.

2. JUVENILES

The custody officer should order the release from detention **unless** he reasonably believes that:

- **any** of the adult criteria above apply or
- it is in the juvenile's own interest

NOTE

This 'own interest' criterion will be rarely used as the adult criteria would normally cover most circumstances. The word 'interest' has a wider meaning than 'own protection' (under the adult criteria) and would include moral, social and educational considerations. Having decided that the juvenile should be detained the question 'where is the most appropriate place for detention?' must be addressed. Should he be detained in local authority accommodation or be kept at the police station? See Chapter 7, Juveniles.

3   If release not required in (1 or 2 above), detention may be authorised.

4   Where authorised, a written record of the detention to be made as soon as practicable.

5   Written record to be made in presence of detainee who at that time shall be told of reasons for detention.

6   5 above does not apply where:

    • Incapable of understanding

    • Violent or likely to be violent

    • In urgent need of medical care.

NOTE ONE

The use of the above criteria serves two functions, ie the duties of the custody officer after charge (section 38 PACE) and the review of police detention by a custody officer (section 40 PACE). Generally custody officers combine these duties, in effect bringing the detention review forward.

NOTE TWO

When a custody officer has sufficient evidence to charge the person with the offence for which he was arrested he shall be charged or released either on bail or without bail. However if the person is not in a fit state to be dealt with, the review officer shall determine whether he is yet in a fit state to be dealt with.

NOTE THREE

The full explanation of bail is contained in Chapter 6, Disposing and Charging.

DIRECTIONS AT VARIANCE WITH THE REVIEW OFFICER

Q What happens if an officer of higher rank gives directions at variance with the decisions or actions taken or contemplated by the review officer?

A1 When that happens the final decision becomes that of the superintendent or above responsible for the police station where the review officer is operating.

HOW TO REVIEW

PACE
S 40 (11)

Q How must the review be carried out?

A2 Free legal advice.

Before a review the review officer must ensure that the prisoner is reminded of his entitlement to free, independent legal advice, using the legal formula detailed below and that the reminder is noted in the custody record.

C
CODE
15.3

NOTE

In addition to the requirement relating to legal advice, the REVIEW OFFICER must record any comment the detainee makes concerning the decision to keep him in detention.

C
CODE
15.2A
& 11.13

The Codes of Practice warn the review officer that any dialogue with the detainee in relation to his comments could constitute an interview and give advice concerning 'unsolicitied comments' by the detainee.

Legal Advice Formula

The person concerned must be told they have a
- Right to FREE and INDEPENDENT legal advice and asked if they want such advice. [The custody officer should make every effort to secure a specific legal advisor, or duty solicitor for the detainee. Further guidance is given in Note 6B].

C
CODE
6.5

If the person declines to speak to a solicitor
- Right to speak to a solicitor on the telephone and asked if he wishes to do so [This conversation should be in PRIVATE, unless the geography of the custody suite makes this impractical.]

NOTE ONE

The explanation of both aspects of this right must be recorded together with the detainee's choices.

NOTE TWO

When a person declines these rights he should be asked the reason and any reason recorded. (Once the detainee has clearly declined both the above, he should not be pressed for his reasons)

A3 Representations (section 40 (12) (13) & (14)).Code C 15.1.

Before deciding on continued detention the review officer shall give the following the opportunity to make representations:

- The prisoner (unless asleep) or
- Any solicitor representing him and available
- A person with an interest in the prisoner's welfare (at the review officers discretion)

Representations may be made orally or in writing, but oral representations from the prisoner may be refused if unfit through his condition or behaviour.

NOTE

Any written representations shall be retained.

A4 Telephone reviews (C Note 15C).

If the only practicable way of conducting a review is over the telephone, then this is permissible, provided:

- Section 40 of PACE (see above) is observed
- If terrorism involved then Schedule 3 Prevention of Terrorism (Temporary Provisions) Act 1989 is observed
- The review **must** be in person when continued detention under section 42 of PACE is reviewed (authorisation of continued detention), see later in this chapter.

> C
> CODE
> 15.5

CUSTODY RECORD – REVIEWS

Must:

- The review officer must record the reasons for any postponement of a review (section.40(7))

- Record the grounds for and extent of any delay in concluding the review (C 15.4)

- Record the fact of reminding the detainee of his entitlement to free legal advice (C15.3)

- Record the outcome of the review as soon as practicable (see also C 15 C above - Telephone Reviews)

C CODE 15.6

Advise to record:

- The date and time of the review

- The identity of the review officer

- Any decision by the superintendent in charge of the station at variance with the intentions, decision or actions of the review officer

- When a review is brought forward to allow the detainee a suitable period of sleep

- The grounds for detention and the circumstances justifying the decision taken

C CODE 15.5

- Any representations received, the person making them and the manner in which they were made (all written representations should be retained)

- Any refusal to hear oral representations and the grounds for that decision

- Why a telephone review was necessary

Example:

1700 hrs   Inspector Pullan's review (prisoner not charged) Second review (9 hours after first).

Informed by PS Harper as to free, independent legal advice in person and on the telephone, and his right to make representations.

Prisoner requests that Inspector Pullan contacts his solicitor, Mr Moore, prior to review.

1710hrs   Solicitor contacted and had no objections to detention. Review conducted by telephone with Inspector Pullan (as only inspector on duty and called to serious road accident).

Review officer's decision to keep in custody to secure and preserve evidence of the offence for which arrested.

The outcome of an interview with a witness due shortly and this evidence to be then put to the suspect. Suspect informed of the review and the grounds for that decision by PS Harper.

LIMITATIONS ON POLICE DETENTION

Q   Who is subject to formal limitations on the time they may be detained?

A   A person arrested for 'an offence' only.

NOTE ONE

'An offence' includes an arrest following a positive breath test or the failure to provide a specimen of breath under the Road Traffic Act.

PACE
S 34

NOTE TWO

People who are not subject to any formal time limit for detention under PACE include:

- Persons arrested under common law powers, eg for a breach of the peace
- Persons arrested and detained under the Mental Health Act.

NOTE THREE

Other categories of persons outside the formal limits of detention under PACE include:

- Persons arrested on a warrant
- Person arrested and detained for other agencies, such as the immigration service, or the armed services etc, not for an offence, but to facilitate other procedures, eg examination, investigation or deportation or return.

Time limits for such detention are contained in other legislation and enquiries should be made with the agencies concerned. (See Chapter 7 on Special Groups).

THE CONTINUOUS REVIEW

It is the responsibility of the custody officer in respect of all prisoners arrested for an offence to maintain a constant review of their detention.

PACE
S 34(2)

The grounds for the review are simply that if at any time a custody officer:

- Becomes aware that the grounds for detention have ceased, and
- Is not aware of any other grounds to justify detention

then he should order the immediate release from custody (either on bail or unconditionally) except for a person who appears to be unlawfully at large at the time of arrest.

NOTE

Persons unlawfully at large include:

- Escapees from lawful custody
- Persons released on prison licence which has been revoked
- Abscondees from mental health custody
- Bail abscondees or those who break bail conditions
- Absentees or deserters from HM Forces.

AUTHORISING RELEASE

PACE
S 34(3)

Only a custody officer can authorise the release of anyone in police detention. The custody officer must be the one currently responsible for the detainee.

PACE
S 34(5)

RELEASE WITH OR WITHOUT BAIL

Where the custody officer bceomes aware that there are no longer grounds for detention the person shall be released unconditionally (without bail) unless it appears to the custody officer:

(a) That further investigation of anything concerning the detention is necessary, or

(b) That proceedings may be instituted against him.

NOTE

If (a) or (b) applies he shall be released on bail.

Detained without charge

Q How long can a person be detained without charging him?
A The answer to that depends on a number of factors and can be up to 96 hours, in special circumstances. However generally the period is 24 hours from the relevant time.

LIMITS ON THE PERIOD OF DETENTION

This section should be read in conjunction with sections 42, 43, and 44 containing the provisions relating to:

PACE
S 41(1)

- Authorising continued detention
- Warrants of further detention and
- Extensions of warrants of further detention.

This section states that a person shall not be kept in police detention for more than 24 hours, without being charged.

PACE
S 41(1)
& (7)

24 hours after the start of relevant time a person in police detention shall be released, either on bail or unconditionally (without bail).

A superintendent can authorise continued detention for up to 36 hours (section.42). Thereafter a magistrates court, can issue a warrant(s), for further detention for up to 96 hours (section.43, 44), but only for serious arrestable offences.

PACE
S 41(8)

Once again these provisions refer to uncharged prisoners.

A person released at the expiry of 24 hours shall not be re-arrested without a warrant for the previous offence unless new evidence warranting his arrest is discovered.

PACE
S 41(9)

NOTE ONE
The investigating officer must discover new evidence after release of a sufficiency to justify the re-arrest for the original offence, at which point a new period of relevant time is initiated.

NOTE TWO
A common problem with investigating officers is to run the enquiry dangerously close to the end of the 24 hour period and then bail the prisoner.

On his return there is not enough relevant time remaining to resolve any ambiguity or develop any lines of enquiry from the earlier interviews. It is not uncommon to bail prisoners with only half an hour or one hour of relevant time remaining.

RELEVANT TIME

PACE
S 41(2)

Q What is meant by 'relevant time?'

A It is the starting point for calculating the period of detention. Unfortunately there are 5 different starting points depending upon the nature of the arrest.

PACE
S 41(2)d

Option 1 The general case

This covers the vast majority of persons in police detention.

Relevant time: the time at which the person arrested arrives at the first police station to which he is taken after arrest.

Option 2 Arrests at the police station

PACE
S 41(2)c

In the case of a person who either:
- Attends voluntarily at the police station, or
- Accompanies a constable to the police station without having been arrested, and is arrested at the police station.

The relevant time is the time of arrest.

Option 3 Arrested outside England and Wales

The relevant time is either:

A At the first police station, in the police area in England and Wales where the offence arrested for is being investigated, or

PACE
S 41(2)b

B The time, 24 hours after the time of that person's entry into England and Wales

Whichever comes first.

Example

An example of option three – Mr X is wanted for an offence committed in Paddington Green, London. He is arrested in Glasgow. Officers from London collect the man and enter England at 1400 hours. He is lodged at New Scotland Yard for an administrative purpose en route to Paddington Green Police Station at 2200 hours the same day. They arrive at Paddington Green at 23.30.

Relevant time would commence at 22.00, when he was lodged at New Scotland Yard, as both police stations are in the Metropolitan Police area where the offence is being investigated.

Had he not arrived at a Metropolitan Police station for 24 hours from entering England or Wales, the relevant time would have started at 1400 hours the following day, ie 24 hours after entry.

Option 4 Arrested solely on behalf of 'our' force

PACE
S 41(2)a
& 41(3)

He is wanted in one police area in England and Wales and he is arrested in another police area, **and**

He is not questioned in the area in which he is arrested for the purpose of obtaining evidence of the offence for which he was arrested.

The relevant time is either:

- **A** The time of arrival
  At the relevant police station
  Within the force where his arrest was sought.
  (ie the first police station taken to in 'our' force)

- or **B** The time
  24 hours after
  The time of arrest

Whichever comes first.

Example

An example of option four – Mr Y is wanted for an offence of theft in Hull, Humberside and he is circulated nationally as wanted. Following a routine check he is arrested in Torquay, Devon, for the Hull offence only.

Humberside police collect Mr Y from Devon and return to Humberside. The first police station they pass in Humberside is Goole, where they decide to lodge the prisoner, whilst the escort has lunch. On arrival at Goole police station the clock has started, much to the annoyance of the Hull detective in charge of the case.

If it had taken longer than 24 hours to collect the prisoner and return to Hull, the clock would have started en route, 24 hours after the arrest. If Devon and Cornwall police had started to question Mr Y on behalf of Humberside Police the relevant time clock would have started ticking.

PACE
S 41(5)

Option 5 Arrested by another force and subsequently arrested on behalf of 'our' force.

If a person is in police detention in a police area in England and Wales (the first area) and he is wanted in some other police area in England and Wales (the second area), and he is taken to the second area to investigate that offence without being questioned in the first area for the purpose of obtaining evidence in relation to it:

The relevant time is either:

    A The time 24 hours after he leaves the police station in the first area

or **B** The time at which he arrives
       at the first police station to which he is taken in the second area

Whichever comes first.

Example

An example of option five – Mr Z is arrested in Manchester by PC Oliver James Dickinson for handling stolen property. He is taken

to the central Bridewell. After his arrest, a routine check revealed that he was wanted in Dover for robbery. He is then arrested by Greater Manchester Police on behalf of the Dover officers.

He is questioned by the Greater Manchester Police about the handling but not about the robbery. Enquiries for the handling offence are completed. He is detained for transfer to Dover.

Dover officers collect Mr Z and return to Kent calling at Canterbury police station where the prisoner is lodged briefly.

The relevant time will normally start at Canterbury as this was the first police station he was taken to in Kent. (Unless it takes more than 24 hours to reach Canterbury from Manchester).

NOTE

In practice the actual arrangements are often determined by investigative or other resource considerations.

The first force could question on behalf of the second force to expedite matters. Papers could be faxed rather than the prisoner moved.

The prisoner could be dealt with by the first force and then bailed to the second force.

On other occasions prisoners are charged and remanded in custody for other offences.

The key to a successful outcome, upon receipt of information that a person has been arrested on your behalf, is consultation and liaison between the investigating officers. They should determine the best course of action, taking into account PACE considerations.

The real danger is to start the clock inadvertently by questioning the prisoner about the secondary offence.

C
CODE
14.1

QUESTIONING IN TRANSIT

Where a person is arrested by force A on behalf of force B and the lawful period of detention in respect of that offence has yet to start in accordance with section 41 PACE, no questions may be asked about the offence whilst travelling between forces except to clarify any voluntary statement made by him.

PACE
S 41(6)

REMOVAL TO HOSPITAL

Q   *When the prisoner is removed to hospital for medical treatment when is relevant time temporarily halted?.*

A   From the time of leaving the 'place of detention' to the time of his return from hospital, the only time which counts towards relevant time is any time during which he is questioned (in relation to obtaining evidence of an offence)

either   i   At the hospital, or
ii   On the way there or back.

NOTE

Generally taking a person to hospital represents time-out, temporarily stopping the time clock from the moment he leaves the police station until the time he returns, provided he is not questioned about any offence for the purpose of obtaining evidence.

PACE
S 118

APPEARANCE AT COURT

Persons appearing at a court, after charge, are not classed as being in police detention, effectively stopping the relevant time clock.

NOTE

Problems arise in relation to a suspect detained for the investigation of offences, who is also required at court. This is a grey area requiring a common sense approach and we suggest the following point, may assist:

- Discuss the case with the C.P.S., the suspect's representative (legal or otherwise) and the investigating officer.
- If the suspect is required at court, arrange an appointment and provide an escort to ensure a secure return to the police station and minimum loss of relevant time.

CHECK LIST – RELEVANT TIME

Key questions

- Is this the first police station the prisoner has been brought to?

- Was the prisoner questioned about the offence for which he is detained before he arrived (at any place or en route)?

- Where was he first arrested?

- Why was he arrested?

- How long did it take to get to the police station after his arrest?

- When did he leave the first police station he was taken to after arrest?

- When did he enter England or Wales?

NOTE

The main principles are:
- The 24 hour rule
- The importance of the first station
- The absence of any questioning.

CUSTODY RECORD – RELEVANT TIME

Advise to record:

- The starting point of the relevant time

- The name of any other police station from which the prisoner has been transferred

- Any relevant timings relating to the transfer

- That the Codes of Practice have been complied with, or any breach or complaint and action taken, eg any questioning of the prisoner about the offence whilst en route

- Any time during which the prisoner was not in police detention, ie in the custody of a court or when relevant time was stopped, eg a hospital visit

Example

1135 hrs   The prisoner arrived at this police station at 1115 hours today. He was arrested for criminal damage at 1100 hours today at St Georges Square.

The Codes of Practice have been complied with and he was not questioned on his way to the station about any offence.

CONTINUED AND FURTHER DETENTION

PACE
S 42

The detention of prisoners beyond 24 hours requires authorisation by a superintendent. This further detention can be for up to 36 hours after relevant time. An extra period of up to 6 hours may be available in which to produce the person before a magistrates' court, ie if the 36 hours period finishes in the early hours of the morning.

PACE
S 43
& 44

After that a further detention must be authorised by a warrant issued by a magistrates' court. The first period should not be longer than 36 hours. Any extension of the warrant should not be longer than 36 hours, or end later than 96 hours after the relevant time.

In practice the custody officer assumes the role of adviser, consultant and arranger between all the parties concerned. He should have a good understanding of the procedures in relation to:

- A superintendent's authorisation

- Warrants of further detention and extension thereto.

Other essential knowledge includes the timing of the relevant reviews, applications to magistrates' courts and the concept of the 'serious arrestable offence'.

AUTHORISATION OF CONTINUED DETENTION

Q What are the key elements of procedure for obtaining an 'authorisation for continued detention?'

PACE
S 42(1)

A A superintendent or above responsible for the police station where the person detained has reasonable grounds for believing:

- That continued detention without charge

- Is necessary to secure or preserve evidence of offence arrested for, or

- To obtain such evidence by questioning.

- Under arrest for a serious arrestable offence; **and**

- Investigation is diligent and expeditious; **then**

- He may authorise further detention for up to 36 hours after relevant time.

NOTE ONE
The review must be authorised in person

NOTE TWO
See Schedule 3, Prevention of Terrorism (Temporary Provisions) Act 1989 for terrorist offences

NOTE THREE
The review must be in person when continued detention under PACE section 42 is reviewed

NOTE FOUR
The powers of a superintendent or above can be exercised by a chief inspector if he has been so authorised by a superintendent or above. (Section 107)

NOTE FIVE
It is not usual for superintendents to grant a full 12 hours extension together with the first 24 hours after relevant time. It is permissible to grant shorter periods provided that when added together they do not expire more than 36 hours after relevant time. (Section 42(2))

165

NOTE SIX

When a prisoner is bailed to a police station the following options exist when he reattends:

(a) To charge

(b) To restart the clock from zero on the basis that new evidence has been discovered of a sufficiency to rearrest him

(c) To question or conduct procedures to secure or preserve evidence within the remaining period of relevant time

(d) To release him.

NOTE SEVEN

It is possible to continue with any 'unused' time from his previous detention when it has exceeded the 24 hour period, ie the superintendent authorised a further 6 hours of continued detention prior to bailing the prisoner to return to the police station. When he returns a superintendent can grant a further 6 hours of continued detention. The use of remaining time also applies to further periods of detention granted by a court.

PACE
S 42(6)
to (8)

NOTE EIGHT

Care must be taken in the wording of such an extension of detention, especially if the superintendent granting it does so before the expiry of 24 hours. It must clearly state when the extension begins and ends otherwise the clock may be viewed as starting from the moment of authorisation.

NOTE NINE

Remember too that the normal reviews carried out by an inspector must continue during the period of extension.

REPRESENTATIONS

Before authorising detention, the officer shall give the detainee, or his solicitor, or his appropriate adult an opportunity to make representations about the detention (section 42(6)) (C.15.1 or 15.2). Other persons having an interest in his welfare may make representations at the review officer's discretion.

These representations can be oral or in writing. Any written representations shall be retained (section 42(7)).

The officer can refuse to hear oral representations from the detainee if he considers him unfit through his condition or behaviour (section 42(8)).

Where continued detention is authorised and the detainee has not yet exercised his right:

- To have someone informed of his arrest, or
- To free independent legal advise, then

    The officer should inform him of these rights and decide whether to permit them (section 42(9)), using the legal advice formula detailed below:

LEGAL ADVICE FORMULA

The person concerned must be told he has a
- Right to FREE and INDEPENDENT legal advice and asked if he wants such advice. [The custody officer should make every effort to secure a specific legal advisor, or duty solicitor for the detainee. Further guidance is given in Note 6B].

If the person declines to speak to a solicitor
- Right to speak to a solicitor on the telephone and asked if he wishes to do so [this conversation should be in PRIVATE, unless the geography of the custody suite makes this impractical].

167

NOTE ONE

The explanation of both aspects of this right must be recorded together with the detainee's choices.

NOTE TWO

When a person declines these rights he should be asked the reason and any reason recorded. (Once the detainee has clearly declined both the above, he should not be pressed for his reasons)

The reminder to free legal advice and the officer's decision or refusal should be recorded in the custody record (C.15.3).

RELEASE

PACE
S 42(10) &
42(11)

Where a person is kept in continued detention, after a superintendent or above's authorisation he shall be released on bail or without bail, not later than 36 hours after the relevant time unless:

PACE
S 43

- He has been charged with an offence, or

- Continued detention authorised or otherwise permitted by a 'warrant of further detention'.

NOTE

Once the prisoner is released he cannot be rearrested for the same offence unless new evidence is discovered after his release of a sufficiency to justify a further arrest.

TIMING OF AUTHORISATIONS

PACE
S 42(4)

Q *When do variations and considerations need to be taken into account for the timing of a superintendent's authorisation?*

A No authorisation for continued detention shall be given before the second review of detention, about 15 hours after detention was first authorised or after 24 hours from the relevant time (normally considered near to the 24 hour point).

NOTE

PACE further advises that if:

PACE
S 43(3)

- It is proposed to transfer the detained person to another police area and any officer is considering authorising continued detention, he should have regard to the time and distance involved.

- The detained person is likely to be asleep at the latest time when a review of detention may take place, the officer authorising continued detention should bring it forward. This allows for representations to be made without interfering with the detainee's period of sleep.

C
CODE
15A

WARRANTS FOR FURTHER DETENTION

Q What are the key elements in the procedures in relation to warrants of further detention?

PACE
S 43(1)

A • An application on oath

- To a magistrates' court

- Supported by an information (see s.43(14) later)

- By a constable, **then**

- The court may issue a warrant of further detention

- When satisfied

- There are reasonable grounds for believing

- The further detention is justified

NOTE ONE
The court may not hear the application unless the:

- Detainee has been given a copy of the information, and

- Is present at court for the hearing.

PACE
S 43(2)

NOTE TWO
The detainee is entitled to legal representation at the hearing and the court can adjourn to enable this. He can be kept in police detention during the adjournment.

PACE
S 42(3)

Comment

**PACE
S 43(4)**

Warrants of further detention are only justified where:

- His detention without charge is necessary

- To secure or preserve evidence of offence arrested for or to obtain such evidence by questioning

- Under arrest for a serious arrestable offence

- Investigation is diligent and expeditious.

WHEN TO APPLY

**PACE
S 43(5)
to 43(9)**

Q When can the application for a warrant for further detention be made?

A At any time up to 36 hours after the relevant time, **or**

Where it is not practicable for the court to sit at the expiry of 36 hours, then the application can be made for up to 6 hours after the 36 hours.

Where the 6 hour period is used the detainee can be kept in police custody during that period. The custody officer shall record that he was kept over 36 hours and the reason why.

Where the application is made after the 36 hour period and the police have no reasonable excuse for not making it before, then the court shall dismiss the application.

Where the court is not satisfied that further detention is justified it can:

- Refuse the application, or

- Adjourn the hearing until a time not later than 36 hours after the relevant time.

In effect this provision gives the police the 36 hours from the start of relevant time as the detainee can be kept in police detention during this adjournment.

LENGTH OF FURTHER DETENTION

**PACE
S 43(10)
to(12)**

Q How long will the warrant authorise further detention?
A Not longer than 36 hours

- The warrant will show how long and state the time at which it was issued.

- The period of detention shall be what the court thinks fit having regard to the evidence before it. Therefore it is important to show good, substantial reasons to satisfy the court.

PACE
S 43(13)

TRANSFER

Where it is necessary to transfer the detainee to another police area at the time of the court hearing, then the court shall have regard to the distance and time of the journey, eg if the journey is estimated as 4 hours then the court may give an extra 4 hours provided the 36 hours is not exceeded. Obviously the police applicant should be aware of the distance and estimated time of the journey at the hearing.

INFORMATION

An information submitted in support of an application for a warrant of further detention shall include:

PACE
S 43(14)

- The nature of the offence
- General nature of the evidence
- Inquiries made and proposed by police
- Reason why continued detention necessary for further inquiries.

REFUSED APPLICATION

PACE
S 43(15)-
(17)

When an application is refused the detainee should be charged or released, with or without bail.

Comment

He need not be released before 24 hours after the relevant time, or before the end of any longer period for which continued detention had been authorised under section 42 above by a superintendent.

No further application is allowed after refusal unless supported by evidence discovered since the refusal.

EXPIRY OF WARRANT

PACE
S 43
(18 & 19)

Q   What happens when a warrant of further detention expires?
A   The detainee shall be released with or without bail, upon or before the expiry, unless he is charged.

Once released he shall not be rearrested for that offence unless new evidence justifying a further arrest is discovered since his release.

EXTENSION OF WARRANT OF FURTHER DETENTION

PACE
S 44

The granting of extensions is similar to 'warrant of further detention' under section.43 PACE. A 'warrant of further detention' may be extended for up to 36 hours or for up to 96 hours after the 'relevant time'. Section 43(2)(3) and (14) ante apply to this section. Where the extension is refused he should be charged or released with or without bail unless there is any detention time left on a previous 'warrant of further detention' or an extension.'

ARRANGING FOR COURT APPEARANCE

Q   Who arranges for the detainee to go to court at the correct time?
A   In practice it is the role of the custody officers to watch the clock and, albeit indirectly, make the arrangements for getting the detainee to court. This is especially so 'out of hours'.

C
CODE
Note 15 B

The application for a warrant of further detention or its extension should be made between 1000 hours and 2100 hours and where possible during normal court hours.

Where possible the justices, clerk should be given notice (during a court sitting) that a special sitting might be needed, ie:

- At weekends
- Bank/public holidays, or
- Weekdays outside normal court hours (but between 1000 hours and 2100 hours)

There is a 6 hours leeway to enable arrangements to be made out of court hours. Beware of section.43(7)(b) where the court will dismiss an application after the 36 hours (even if in the 6 hours leeway) if the police could have brought it during the 36 hours, but failed to do so.

NOTE

Unexpired time from a superintendent or the court can be used for a suspect who is police bailed and then re-detained. When the remaining time has expired, further extensions must be sought if it is desired to still detain him.

CUSTODY RECORD – AUTHORISATION
OF CONTINUED DETENTION

Must

- Record the grounds for the prisoner's continued detention (section 42(5)(b))

- Record any decision and the grounds for any refusal to allow access to legal advice (section 42(9)(b)).

Advise to record

- Name and rank of officer authorising continued detention

- Time of authorisation

- Any special reasons for the timing, eg prisoner about to sleep

- The offence for which the prisoner's detention is to continue

- The grounds for regarding it as a serious offence.

- The names of the officers with whom the authorising officer consulted

- A short précis of the information they provided to the authorising officer

- The timing of the content, the manner of making and the identity of the person making representations

- Any refusal to hear oral representations and the reasons for it

- Any arrangement made to allow a written representation

> A record that he was informed of his entitlement to free independent legal advice and access to legal advice by telephone.
> The period of time for which the continued detention was authorised.

CUSTODY RECORD – WARRANTS FOR FURTHER DETENTION

Must

Record the time the prisoner was kept in detention whilst arrangements were made and the reason why he was so kept, when not practical to bring the prisoner before a court within 36 hours after relevant time.

Record the outcome of any application.

Advise to record

The service of the copy of the 'information' on the prisoner

Any arrangements made to produce the prisoner before the court

Where the application was made after 36 hours, the reasons why it was not practicable to make the application within the relevant time

The period of further detention granted, or period of extension, or further extension

Where the warrant was refused and the person was kept in police detention, the period of time remaining or authorised

Any period of detention during an adjournment to obtain legal representation.

Example

0530   The 36 hours expired at 0530 hours today. No court available until 1000 hours today.
Long and complex interviews followed by sleep precluded an appearance at court within the 36 hours.

1030   Application successful for further detention for 25 hours.
Prisoner produced before Sometown Magistrates' Court at 1000 hours and a warrant of further detention issued for 25 hours.
Prisoner to be returned before court tomorrow for 1000 hours for further consideration.
Warrant ref 123/92 attached hereto.

Chapter 6
DISPOSAL & CHARGING

This chapter considers charging procedures and the ways in which a detainee can leave detention. It examines these matters from the custody officer's perspective.

Q How can a person who has been arrested for an offence leave the custody suite?

A1 Bailed:

    i) To a police station

    ii) After charge to a court

    iii) After being arrested on a warrant backed for bail.

A2 Taken before a court in custody.

A3 Released unconditionally, but could be cautioned or reported for summons.

A4 Transferred to another's custody.

NOTE

PACE
S 39 (2)

A person may also leave the custody of the custody officer on a temporary basis to:

- an officer investigating the offence, ie to interview or for an identification parade;
- an officer outside the police station, ie to recover property, be involved in a search or be taken for medical treatment.

In these cases the duties and responsibilities of the custody officer are transferred to the officer concerned.

CHARGING

C
CODE
16.1

Q When should a detained person be charged with an offence?

A   The legal criteria necessary for this decision to be made are contained in the PACE Codes of Practice:

1   When an officer considers that there is sufficient evidence to prosecute the detained person;
   and

2   there is sufficient evidence for a prosecution to succeed;
   and

3   the person has said all he wishes to say about the offence;
   then

   that person should be brought before the custody officer without delay.

The custody officer is responsible for deciding whether he should be charged.

OPTIONS

*Q Given that all the above criteria are fulfilled is charging the
only option available?*

A There are other considerations outside the Codes of Practice
which a custody officer should quite properly take into
account in considering whether a person might be charged. In
practice there are always three options open to him.

Option 1: Charge the detained person

NOTE
See the options available after charge, post.

Option 2: Report – Report the detained person for summons

This option is particularly suited to minor crimes or situations
where a caution or no further action would suffice, eg juveniles,
persons suffering physical or mental illness etc.

Option 3: Bail – Bail the detained person for a decision

NOTE
This is the best course of action when it is doubtful that
the evidence is sufficient for a prosecution to succeed,
or there is some doubt as to the appropriate charge.

MULTIPLE OFFENCES

*Q Is it possible to delay charging a
detained person who is in custody for
multiple offences?*

A Yes, the choice depends on the probable
time scale of the investigation and the
attendant circumstances. Essentially the
decision rests on the necessity principle.

Option A: Charging criteria fulfilled

It is permissible to delay charging the
prisoner until all the charging criteria (see
above) are fulfilled for each of the offences
concerned.

C
CODE
16.1

Comment

This course of action is advised where it seems probable that the investigation into all the offences will be resolved in a relatively short time scale.

This includes those occasions where a detention period beyond 24 hours is contemplated, provided serious arrestable offences are involved.

In general this option is preferred to resolve clearing up multiple offences from a cooperative detainee. It also allows the custody officer to determine the most appropriate package of charges and offences taken into consideration, etc.

Option B: Charge and Remand

It may be advisable to charge the detained person with one offence and produce him before a court seeking a remand in custody. The remand could be to prison or to police cells to investigate the outstanding offences.

Comment

In cases where it seems probable that the investigation can be resolved within a medium time scale, ie a three-day remand into police custody requiring instant access to the prisoner may be appropriate. Alternatively when an extended time scale is probable, but the release of the person would be inappropriate, a remand to prison might be required.

One advantage of this option is that by charging the detainee, the relevant time clock is stopped. This eases the time pressure on both suspect and the investigating officer alike. The decision regarding continued detention is taken out of police hands and is placed before the independent magistrate.

Option C: Charge and bail

In this instance the detainee is charged to appear at court some time hence and/or bailed back to the police station for other offences, to a time within the period set for his court appearance. On answering bail the person may be charged with an additional offence(s) prior to attending at court. Alternatively he may be released from his bail obligation by letter to attend court for the original charge only.

Remember to ensure that the detainee has been fully informed of any other offence(s) for which he has been detained by way of a notional arrest for these further offences.

PACE
S 31

Also ensure that once the criteria have been fulfilled for each separate offence, questioning has ceased for that offence.

C
CODE
11.4

WHAT TO CHARGE

Q *How do you determine the appropriate offence with which to charge?*

A There is no easy answer to this question. The most important criterion is that of evidence, without which the charge will fail.

Other considerations

- the likely plea

- the venue

- the outcome in terms of penalty

- the effect of your decision on the victim and the detainee.

NOTE

The 'other considerations' have been formalised to some extent by the ACPO Crime Committee's guidelines entitled 'The Cautioning of Offenders' which some forces have consolidated into specific instructions, eg the Metropolitan Police' 'Case Disposal Manual'. They create a series of gravity factors which are 'offence specific' or 'general', (such as age or pre-meditation) reducing the decision to charge or caution, etc into an arithmetical problem, to reduce subjectivity.

Custody officers should also be aware of HO Circular 18/1994 which provides guidance on the principles and practice of cautioning offenders, advocating common sense and discretion.

Comment

Many officers simply charge the most serious offence the evidence will support. They believe the other considerations are best left to the court. It is suggested that careful thought be given to this area and to illustrate this point the following example is offered under the Public Order Act 1986 section 1:

A group of 20 to 30 football supporters go on the rampage, causing damage, threatening members of the public and causing general harassment, alarm and distress. Technically they fulfill the requirements of a riot. However if charged with this offence, riot damages may be payable by the police. The offence must be tried at Crown Court. The penalty is up to 10 years' imprisonment.

It would be more cost effective if the individuals were charged with various lesser offences, ie minor criminal damage, or sections 4 and 5 of the Public Order Act 1986. If bailed to the same court on the same date they could be adequately punished at the bargain basement magistrates' court prices, thereby saving the taxpayer unnecessary expense.

NOTE

On occasions an offence taken into consideration (TIC) may be more appropriate than an outright charge.

For example a persistent juvenile offender is found committing offences whilst on bail to appear at court in a few days' time. The natural inclination is to charge him with the offence even though it is only a minor offence. Such a charge would add virtually nothing to his punishment and may lead to an adjournment, thereby putting him back into circulation without punishment.

A well placed TIC offence will not prevent him being dealt with expeditiously, whilst informing the youth court of his activities.

REMAND TO POLICE CUSTODY

*Q   What about charges in relation to prisoners remanded into
     police custody?*
A   Once charged with other offences under investigation or
        indeed deemed to be innocent of all wrongdoing, the custody
        officer must ensure that the prisoner is brought before the
        next available court.

PACE
S 34

NOTE

Problems arise when persons remanded into police custody are being investigated for multiple offences. As investigations are completed there is pressure to charge the suspect, leaving other offences outstanding. We advise that charging is delayed until all the investigations are complete, then charge all the outstanding offences. Where it is not possible to complete an investigation within the period of the remand, the strategy of using bail to the police station as a means of continuing enquiries should not be used, as relevant time cannot re-commence when the suspect answers bail. Instead a further remand should be sought, or if the suspect is released by the court, he should be re-arrested if new evidence becomes available justifying arrest, and a new period of relevant time begun.

REVIEW OF EVIDENCE BEFORE CHARGE

*Q   Is it necessary to review all the evidence prior to making a
     decision as to whether to charge the detained person?*
A   In reality it is often impracticable for the custody officer at a
        busy station to view all the evidence, even if it is available.

He must rely on his colleagues to inform and advise him. Often other supervisors and experts will have reviewed the evidence and recommended charging the prisoner. However, the final decision rests with the custody officer who can remain more objective than persons involved in the case. He is able to take a step back and look at the big picture, before making his decision.

Cautioning before Charging/Report for Summons

Having reviewed the evidence for one or more offences and determined to charge/report the suspect with the appropriate offence, the custody should ensure that the officer charging/reporting for summons:

- Cautions the suspect (Code C, 16.2)
- Gives the suspect a written notice showing:
- the offence (in simple terms)
- and pre-faced with the appropriate caution (Code C, 16.3)

NOTE

The cautions relates specifically to charging and has different wording to the 'standard' caution.

CUSTODY RECORD – CHARGING

Advise to record

The general nature of the charge eg theft, handling etc

The officer charging the prisoner

The time and date of the charge

Any other relevant information eg. whether a third party was present – solicitor, appropriate adult or interpreter etc

Example

PACE
S 34 (3)

0945   The prisoner was charged with theft of a twenty pound note by PC Kevin Sharp. His solicitor Mr D Strachan was also present.

signed PS Harper

NOTE

There are special additional provisions in relation to juveniles and persons mentally disordered or mentally handicapped. See Chapter 7 on Special Groups.

DISPOSAL

Introduction

The custody officer constantly reviews each detention, considering several options, as follows:-

- To continue detention in relation to a breach of the peace,or

- To continue detention under the terms of a warrant, or

- To continue detention in accordance with various administrative directions, eg persons detained under immigration legislation, or

- To continue detention for investigative purposes, or

- To continue detention until the person is fit to charge/report, eg under the influence of drink or drugs, or

- To continue detention after charge [see Reviews After Charge Chapter 5 ante], or

- To release the person unconditionally [see post], or

- To bail to a court or to a police station, or

- To transfer to another's custody [see post].

The remainder of this chapter deals with those options involving the act of disposal and their significance to the custody officer.

UNCONDITIONAL RELEASE

Where the custody officer becomes aware that there are no longer grounds for keeping a person in detention, he shall release him unconditionally without bail, unless he considers

PACE
S 34 (5)

- That further investigation of anything concerning the detention is necessary

- That, proceedings may be initiated against him

NOTE

If either condition applies he shall be released **on bail.**

In recent years there has been a marked increase in the number of persons unconditionally released. Persons may be unconditionally released for a number of reasons:

(a) they are believed to be innocent of any wrong-doing;

(b) they are arrested unlawfully;

(c) there were no grounds for detention, ie no necessity to detain them by virtue of the nature of the offence and/or their particular circumstances;

(d) they are not fit for detention, eg releasing a person arrested for a minor offence without conditions who needs hospital admission. This makes logistical sense as it releases an officer from many unproductive hours waiting at the hospital;

(e) after being reported for summons.

NOTE

Although he may be a suitable candidate for bail by virtue of the fact that 'proceedings may be taken against him in respect of any such matter', proceedings by way of summons seem more appropriate as in the case of persons arrested for drink driving.

(f) After charge.

RELEASE AUTHORISATION

Q Who can authorise release?

A Only the custody officer can release a detained person:

PACE
S 34(3)

(1) At the police station where detention authorised

(2) Or if detained at more than one station, where it was last authorised.

BAIL TO A COURT OR POLICE STATION

Introduction

Under the Bail Act 1976, people charged with an offence have, in some circumstances, a universal **right** to bail and in other circumstances **may** be granted bail. PACE generally requires the custody officer to grant bail either:

RELEASE ON BAIL

PACE
S 47

- To a court (section 47(3)(a))

- To a police station (section 47(3)(b))

(**except** where the person has been charged or convicted of murder, attempted murder, rape, attempted rape, or manslaughter and has a previous conviction for any of these offences. (See Criminal Justice and Public Order Act 1994 section 25 for further details; **or** he is accused or convicted of committing an offence while on bail (Bail Act 1976, amended by section 26 Criminal Justice and Public Order Act 1994)).

NOTE

Before granting bail ensure that all the proper checks have been made regarding outstanding warrants, offences or missing/wanted indexes etc.

It is very embarrassing to have bailed a detained person only to discover that he was wanted or missing.

The granting of bail both to a court and to a police station is dealt with under PACE Act 1984 and the Bail Act 1976

Q   What type of bail can a person be granted?

A   There 6 types of bail, namely

(i) Bail under a duty to surrender to custody

(ii) Bail with sureties

(iii) Bail with securities

(iv) Bail with conditions

(v) For juveniles, with a parent or guardian acting as surety, to ensure that he complies with any conditions

(vi) Bail under the terms of a warrant

All these types of bail have one purpose to secure a person's surrender to custody, at a **police station** or to a **court**. However not all the types of bail are applicable to both cases, for example 'bail conditions' can only be imposed when bail is to court.

The following section will explain these types of bail in some depth leading to a diagram comparing bail to a court and bail to police station.

Bail under a duty to surrender to custody. Section 3 Bail Act 1976 (To a court or to a police station)

The majority of detained persons are bailed by being placed under a duty to surrender to custody at the appointed place and time.

NOTE ONE

ABSCONDING
(Bail to a Court)

FAIL TO ANSWER BAIL
(Bail to a Police Station)

If the bailee fails to answer bail to court an offence of absconding is committed [section.6 Bail Act 1976], for which there is a power of arrest, with or without warrant [section.7 Bail Act 1976]. The person arrested must be taken to the next available court in the area in which he was arrested, **UNLESS arrested within 24** hours of the appointed time of surrender, in which case he must be returned to the court to which he was bailed. *[This does not apply to Christmas Day, Good Friday or any Sunday]*

If the bailee fails to answer bail at a police station, an offence of absconding is committed [section 6 Bail Act, 1976], for which there is a power of arrest, section 46A PACE Act 1984. Under this section, the arrested person must be taken, as soon as practicable, to the police station appointed for surrender. The person can then be detained for interview, for securing or preserving evidence, or for charging.

NOTE TWO

Any proceedings, for failing to surrender to custody to a court, or at a police station, should be initiated by charging the accused or laying on information, ie by summons.

Bail with sureties. Sections 3(3) and 8(1) Bail Act 1976

When there is doubt as to a person's own guarantee to surrender to custody, he may be required to provide one or more sureties, before being bailed.

The police, a court or a judge in chambers may require a surety. The following list includes matters which should be taken into account regarding the suitability of a surety:

Financial soundness

- Good character
- Any previous convictions
- Relationship to the bailee, ie blood, friend, neighbour etc
- The willingness and the ability to act as a surety.

Purpose

The custody officers' powers are further 'modified' by section 3A(5) of the Bail Act, 1976, in as much as a sureties can **only** be required if **necessary** for the purpose of preventing a person from:

- Failing to surrender, **or**
- Committing offences on bail, or
- Interfering with witnesses, or
- Obstructing justice

NOTE

A surety is essentially a promise by a person who has some relationship with the detained person to pay a financial forfeit should the bailee fail to appear at the appointed time and place.

Hopefully this guarantees the bailee's attendance because of the 'special' relationship between them.

This procedure does not entail the custody officer taking any money or valuables from the person standing surety.

Bail with securities. Section 3(4) Bail Act 1976

Occasionally it is necessary to take a physical security in the form of money or valuables from the bailee or someone on his behalf. This security would then be forfeited if the bailee fails to turn up at the appointed time and place. This procedure tends to be restricted to bail on directions of a court. Once again the requirement can only made when it is necessary to prevent the person from:

- Failing to surrender
- Committing offences on bail
- Interfering with witness
- Obstructing justice

Bail with conditions. Section 47 PACE Act 1984 and sections 3, 3A, 5 and 5A Bail Act 1976

(To a court only)

Conditions

A custody officer is empowered to demand that a person charged and released [section 38(1) PACE 1984] or having been charged and detained, but later reviewed and released [section 40(10) PACE 1984] submit to conditions prior to release on bail to a court.

There conditions are to ensure that the bailee will:

- Surrender to custody
- Not commit offences on bail
- Not interfere with witnesses
- Not obstruct justice

Any conditions may be imposed to ensure the above (section 3(6) Bail Act 1976), but normally will include those commonly used by the courts, eg qualifications as to residence; visiting premises or places; curfew; approaching people or pemises; or reporting to a police station (check your own force information for further guidance).

NOTE ONE

Custody officers have been granted similar powers to magistrates to impose bail conditions. Fairness and accuracy must be the watchwords when drafting such conditions. Special care should be taken when imposing or varying conditions so that they do not conflict with each other.

NOTE TWO

The bail provisions available to custody officers under section 3 of the Bail 1976 have been strictly limited and the following conditions available only to courts have been excluded from custody officers:

- Requirement to reside at Bail Hostels, etc [section.3(6.2A) Bail Act 1976]
- Examinations of persons charged with murder [section .3(6A) Bail Act 1976]

Variations

Bail conditions can be varied by the custody officer granting bail or another custody officer **at the same police station**. This can only be done at the request of the bailee and new conditions imposed .

NOTE ONE

Custody officers can only vary conditions granted by themselves or other custody officers at their police station. Only a court can vary conditions set by a court.(Though the police can make an application for a variation, or indeed ask the court to revoke bail).

Representations

In practice, solicitors may proffer conditions acceptable to their client, especially in cases where bail is likely to be refused, eg 'Would my client get bail if he agreed to a curfew during the hours of darkness?'

The custody officer may find merit in such suggestions and it is advised that all such representations should be recorded.

Power of Arrest

Under section 7 Bail Act 1976, there is a power of arrest where there are reasonable grounds to believe the bailee has broken, or is likely to breach, any bail conditions imposed by a court or a custody officer. After arrest the bailee must be dealt with in the same manner as an absconder [see 'Bail under a duty to surrender to custody' ante].

Juveniles with a parent or guardian acting as surety
(Section 3(7) Bail Act 1976.)

A custody officer can require a parent or guardian to act as a surety to ensure a juvenile complies with any request to surrender to custody or bail conditions. However this request is limited to:

- Parents of juveniles who have not reached the age of 17 by the time they are required to surrender to bail to a court.

- A maximum surety of £50.

Bail under the terms of a warrant

This is the most straightforward bail of all. The custody officer simply follows the directions of the warrant 'backed for bail' which sets out the conditions under which bail may be granted.

NOTE

It is important that the custody officer checks that the warrant has been properly endorsed by the arresting officer.

It is also advisable to confirm the detained person's details and that the matter dealt with in the warrant is known and understood by the detainee. Any discrepancies should be enquired into, eg warrant is defective.

THE CUSTODY OFFICER AND BAIL

Q What is the role of the custody officer in the process of granting bail?

A The most important functions of the custody officer in relation to bail are:

   1 The granting of bail (as only the custody officer can authorise release of a detained person from custody).
   2 Explain the terms and conditions of bail.

NOTE

Under section 47 PACE 1984, the custody officer can impose bail conditions, or demand parental sureties for juveniles as a pre-requisite to bailing to a court. (See 'Bail with Conditions' and 'Juveniles: Parent or Guardian acting as surety.' ante)

Where a custody officer grants, imposes or varies conditions of bail, he must give the reasons for doing so to the bailee; note the reasons in the custody record and give the bailee a copy in writing). (Sections 5 and 5A Bail Act 1976).

   3 Inform the detained person of the offence of failing to answer to bail and the power of arrest for absconding or breaking conditions of bail.

NOTE ONE

The Bail Act 1976 section 6(1) created the offence of failing to surrender to custody without reasonable cause.

Charging the person with the offence of failing to answer bail will provide evidence to any future custody officer making a decision regarding the granting of bail.

NOTE TWO

Section 46A PACE 1984 created a power of arrest for persons who failed to answer bail to a police station, allowing them to be returned to the 'bailing' station to continue interview, or to preserve evidence, or for charging Under section 47(6) PACE 1984, the relevant-time clock recommences when the arrested person arrives at a police station.

NOTE THREE

This section creates another exception in relation to relevant time, in as much as an arrest for failing to answer bail does not initiate a new period of relevant time under section 47(7) PACE 1984. It appears to re-start the clock when the person is detained at any police station. Obviously, in an ideal situation this will be the station to which the person should have surrendered, but where the person is arrested elsewhere and taken to the nearest station, the time he is detained awaiting transfer would, it appears, count as relevant time, ie re-starting the clock. In the absence of any judicial or Home Office advice, it is our opinion that the provisions under section 41 of PACE (limits on Periods of Detention without Charge) may apply, whereby if the bail absconder is arrested outside the force area (where he was to have surrendered) the relevant time would generally be re-started when he arrives at the first station to which he is taken in that force area; notwithstanding the provisions of section.41 designed to prevent time wasting by the police.

PACE
S 38

NOTE FOUR

Sections 3 and 3A Bail Act 1976 give custody officers the power to impose bail conditions and to require sureties from parents and guardians for persons granted bail after charge or review (sections 38(1) and 40(10) PACE

1984). Again this is supported by a power of arrest.

4   Ensure that all the parties concerned are properly informed by way of written communication or by telephone, ie:

- The detained person

- The officer in the case

- The police station or court concerned.

5   Return the person's property against signature.

CUSTODY RECORD – BAIL

Advise to record

The time and date at which bail was granted

The time, date and place to which the person is bailed to appear

Where bail is granted with conditions, record the reasons for granting, imposing or varying them. Where bail is granted under conditions set out in a warrant, brief details of the warrant, ie date issued, court issuing and any conditions

Example

2010   Prisoner bailed to appear at Sometown Magistrates' Court at 1000 hours on 24.5.92.

ANSWERING BAIL

PACE
S 34(7)

Q   What action does the custody officer take when a person bailed to the police station answers his bail?

A   He may only be detained without charge in connection with that offence where the custody officer has reasonable grounds to believe that detention is necessary:

(a) to secure or preserve evidence relating to the offence, or
(b) to obtain such evidence by questioning him.

Where a person is detained on answering bail or arrested for not answering police bail, any time during which he was in police detention prior to being granted bail shall be included as part of any period which falls to be calculated under this part of PACE.

PACE
S 47(6)

NOTE ONE
In effect releasing the person on bail has stopped the relevant time clock, which is restarted the moment he submits himself back under arrest by answering bail.

NOTE TWO
Nothing in the Bail Act 1976 shall prevent the re-arrest without warrant of a person released on bail subject to a duty to attend at a police station if new evidence justifying a further arrest has come to light since his release. The relevant time clock starts at zero again, provided that such a re-arrest is made before the person answers bail.

PACE
S 47(2)

NOTE THREE
Where a person is released on bail to attend at a police station and is rearrested, the provisions of PACE shall apply as if arrested for the first time, ie full rights entitlements and information.

However if the person released on bail fails to answer bail and is re-arrested, it appears that the relevant time clock recommences when he arrives at the first police station at which he is detained. Ideally this will be the station to which the person should have surrendered, however if he is arrested elsewhere and taken to the nearest police station the time he is detained awaiting transfer would appear to count as relevant time. In the absence of any judicial or Home Office advice, it is our opinion that the provisions under section 41 PACE (limits on periods of detention without charge) may apply;. whereby if the bail absconder is arrested outside the force area (where he was to have surrendered), the relevant time would generally be re-started when he arrives at the first station to which he is taken in that force area not withstanding the provisions in section.41 designed to prevent time wasting by the police.

RELEASING FROM BAIL

PACE
S 47(4)

Q   What happens when it is no longer necessary for a person to answer his bail at a police station?

A   The custody officer may give notice in writing to that person releasing him from his attendance at the police station.

RE-BAIL

Q   Is it possible to re-bail a person to a police station?

A   Whilst some confusion exists it is considered that it is permissible to bail a person more than once back to the police station, without re-arresting him on new evidence. A sufficiency of relevant time must remain.

ADMINISTRATION

Q   What are the administrative procedures associated with releasing a detained person either on bail or by an unconditional release?

A   Always ensure:

The custody record is fully completed.

The detainee has received all the property taken from him against signature.

The cell in which the prisoner has been held, is thoroughly checked for damage, or property left behind.

Any indexes connected with the custody record are completed.

BAIL TO A NON-DESIGNATED POLICE STATION

Difficulties can arise when bailing a person to a Non-Designated Police Station and we advice that when 6 hours of relevant time have elapsed the suspect should only be bailed to a Non-Designated station pending 'a decision', ie when it is anticipated that the suspect will be charged, rather than interviewed further.

REFUSING BAIL

Q *What are the criteria for refusing bail for persons arrested and charged with an offence?*

A Where a person arrested for an offence (other than by warrant endorsed for bail) is charged with an offence, it is presumed that he will be released from police detention, either on bail or without bail, unless:

- Name and address not known, or in doubt; or
- The suspect would fail to answer bail at court; or
- He will interfere with justice or with the investigation; or
- Necessary for the suspects own protection; or

Imprisonable

- Custody officer has reasonable belief that detention necessary to **prevent** him from committing **an offence**, eg known drug addict charged with 'shoplifting' and custody officer has reasonable grounds to believe he would continue shoptlifting regularly to feed his addiction. The reasonable grounds being his admission of living by means of shoplifting and previous offending history (to be recorded on custody record).

Non-Imprisonable

- Custody officer has reasonable belief that detention necessary to **prevent harm** to other person or to property, eg suspect charged with section 5 Public Order Act 1986, causing harassment, alarm or distress to a neighbour and the custody officer has reasonable grounds to believe he will return to the scene and cause damage or injure the victim.

The reasonable grounds being his threat to throw a brick through the window at the victim (to be entered on the custody record).

NOTE

It is expected that the majority of persons detained will have been charged with imprisonable offences. Only rarely will the more limited criteria under 'non-imprisonable offences' be required to detain the suspect after charge.

Juveniles

The custody officer should order the release from detention **unless** he reasonably believes that:

- **any** of the adult criteria above apply or
- it is in the juvenile's own interest.

NOTE

This 'own interest' criterion will be rarely used as the adult criteria would normally cover most circumstances. The word 'interest' has a wider meaning than 'own protection' (under the adult criteria) and would include moral, social and educational considerations.

The decision rests with the custody officer. He must have reasonable grounds for believing the appropriate criteria apply to the detained person. Each case must be considered on its merits and indivdual decisions will be reviewable by the courts.

Comment

PACE
S 39(6)

In practice the decision **not** to grant bail is often hotly contested. The custody officer should gather together the grounds for a reasonable belief to support one or more of the criteria. It is rare for this decision to go to the arbitration of the superintendent responsible for the station.

Section 25 of the Criminal Justice and Public Order Act 1994 now provides that certain offences do not attract bail either from the police or a court where the suspect has been charged with such an offence and has a previous conviction for such an offence (murder, manslaughter rape and attempts).

CUSTODY RECORD – BAIL REFUSED

Must record

PACE
38(3) &
38(4)

The grounds of the detention as soon as practicable

This record shall be made in the presence of the person charged. He shall be informed by the custody officer of the grounds for his detention;

Unless at the time the written record is made he is:

incapable of understanding

violent or likely to become violent or

in urgent need of medical attention.

Advise to record

The reason(s) for forming the reasonable grounds for the custody officer's belief

C
CODE
1.1

The purpose for which the detained person is being placed before the court

Remand to police cells

Remand to prison

Example

0815 Bail refused for fear of violence to his wife. Recorded in absence of defendant who is still displaying aggression and violence to all police staff.

Witnesses and the officer in the case have all heard the defendant threaten to kill his wife. This has given me reasonable grounds to believe his detention is necessary to prevent injury to his wife.

A remand to prison is to be applied for in view of next court date.

GOING TO COURT

*Q What are the administrative procedures associated with
taking a person to court when in custody?*

A Always check that:

The custody record is complete

The custody record or a copy accompanies the detainee to
court, (depending on your own force procedures)

Any relevant warrant or certificate under Code C 16.9 for
a juvenile, is sent with him

Any 'exceptional risk' form is attached to the prisoner's
record

The property (preferably still sealed) is handed to the
escorting officer

Both the detainee and his property are handed over
against signature by the escorting officer.

The escort should be suitable for the safety and security of the detained person.

- Any medication brought by or obtained for the detainee, accompanies him.

- The cell in which he was detained is checked for any damage or property left behind.

- Any indexes used in conjunction with the custody record are completed.

TRANSFER OF PRISONERS

Q   What are the procedures for the transfer of prisoners?
A   Detained person can be transferred to the following secure accommodation:

other police stations within the force area or to another force area;

to prison, detention centre etc;

to some other agency, ie immigration, armed services, etc;

to a mental institution (premises sanctioned under the Mental Health Act);

to social service accommodation (juveniles).

Generally the procedure is the same with specific variations relating to the receiving organisation.

An area of concern, is the 'short term commitment warrant' og 7 days to prison for non-payment of fine. Street-wise prospective prisoners, knowing that the 7 days will be reduced and that prisons do not release prisoners over the weekend, are lining up at custody suites on Thursdays, as near as possible to 11.55 pm.

Subsequent discussions between custody officers and prisons often end with the custody officer releasing the prisoner on Friday. In the absence of any force policy, we would advocate that custody officers engaging in the practice, fax the warrant and details of the prisoner to the prison and receive a return fax authorising release. It pays to be safe.

The following check list should assist the custody officer to cover all the necessary procedures:

CHECK LIST – TRANSFER OF PRISONERS

1 Contact the receiving point and ensure the prisoner will be accepted.

2 Examine the detained person's condition prior to transfer and check that it matches his condition on arrival. Any charge should be recorded in the custody record.

3 Ensure that the custody record is fully completed and either the record or a copy accompanies the prisoner. (Depending on your force procedure).

4 Attach to the custody record any exceptional risk forms or warrants etc.

5 Always check whether warrant conditions can be fulfilled to prevent commitment to prison eg payment of outstanding money or fine arrears etc.

6 Ensure that the detained person and his property are handed over to the senior escorting officer against signature.

Certain institutions such as prisons will not accept items of personal property, eg cameras, stop watches, or ornate rings with 'stones' etc. It is good practice to obtain a detailed list of acceptable items. Unacceptable property can then be handed over to friends or relatives against the detainee's signature.

Alternatively the property could be entered into police property for safekeeping, collection or other disposal.

NOTE

Prisons and similar establishments require that property accompanying a detained person is entered in the HM Body Receipt Book, which should be sent with the prisoner, in order that the prison can signify receipt. The book is then returned to the appropriate station.

7   Any medication brought by or obtained for the detainee should accompany him.

8   Ensure that the cell in which he was detained is checked for any damage or any hidden or discarded property.

9   Ensure that any indexes used in conjunction with the custody record are properly completed.

10 Endorse the custody record to show where the prisoner was transferred, the time, date and reason.

NOTE

Ensure that the escort is suitable for the safety and security of the detained person.

Additional procedures are applicable to juveniles (see Chapter 7 Special Groups).

PRIVATE ESCORT SERVICES

Private 'prisoner custody officers' (PCO's) are provided for under the Criminal Justice Act 1991, such as Group 4 Court Escort Services Ltd. Forces have their own policy document for such contractors but briefly PCO's are responsible for:

- Keeping their own custody records

- preventing escape

- reporting on any unlawful acts

- good order, discipline and prisoners' well being

- following court directions for prisoners' treatment.

PCO's will transport, all prisoners too and from court except high security category prisoners (see force policy),(juveniles from court to places of detention other than prison police stations,) prisoners from court to psychiatric hospitals and prisoners from operation 'container' or similar operations.

Handover procedures:

- visible injuries/complaints of other injury – the custody officer should give PCO written confirmation of that fact

- PCO is responsible for prisoner's property once bag seals are checked against records.

- Property not acceptable by prisons should not be given to PCO's – endorse custody record.

- PCO's to sign custody record re prisoner and property.

The PCO should be given, where appropriate, any warrant, 'prisoner exceptional risk form', any other appropriate records or documents for court, and any medication details.

NOTE

It is important for the custody officer to ensure that the PCO is informed of any medication given or to be given and any appropriate medical directions. The passing of such information should be noted on the custody record.

Chapter 7
SPECIAL GROUPS

SPECIAL GROUPS

Juveniles and children in police protection

Mentally disordered and mentally handicapped persons

The 'appropriate adult'

Blind, deaf, unable to read, speak, or understand English

Illegal immigrants/foreign nationals

Wards of court

Less common 'Special Groups' and where to find the relevant
information are shown below:

1 Terrorist suspects

> The Prevention of Terrorism Acts

> PACE Act sections 56(11), 58(13), 61(9), 64(7), 116(5)
> and Schedule 2

> Codes of Practice (Indexed under the Prevention of
> Terrorism)

2 Armed forces (PACE Act section 113 – application to armed
forces and Schedule 2, preserved powers)

3 Persons sentenced to police cells (See Magistrates' Courts
Act 1980, sections 135 (detention for one day at a police station)
and 136 (committal to overnight custody at a police station)).

JUVENILES

(See also wards of court, post)

Q *What special provisions apply to the arrest, detention, and
conditions of treatment of juveniles?*

A Children and young persons come into the police station in
one of two ways, either as arrested persons, under the
provisions of PACE Act 1984, or for their protection, under
the provisions of the Children Act 1989.

TAKING CHILDREN INTO POLICE PROTECTION

Under the Children Act 1989 a child (any person under the age of
18 years) may be taken into police protection where the constable
has reasonable cause to believe:

> that a child might suffer significant harm ('harm' means ill
> treatment or the impairment of health or development);

> that the child may be removed from any hospital or other
> place where he is being accommodated.

A police station is not considered as being suitable
accommodation under the Act. Ideally he should be taken directly
to the local authority. The custody officer should inform the
constable of this fact before he arrives at the police station.

Short stays at the police station may be unavoidable. However, the Children Act requires the local authority to provide such accommodation.

PACE does not apply. Children taken into police protection are NOT under arrest and the Codes of Practice and custody records do not apply. Cell accommodation should only be used in extreme cases.

Individual force standing orders will cover some of the above areas and should be consulted.

Treating as a juvenile

Q When should a person be treated as a juvenile for the purpose of the PACE Act and the Codes of Practice?

A Anyone apparently under 17 shall be treated as a juvenile, in the absence of clear evidence to show he is older.

C
CODE
1.5

Therefore a person who is 17 should be dealt with as an adult under the PACE Act and the Codes of Practice.

D
CODE
1.4

NOTE

The Children and Young Persons Act, 1933 (as amended by the Criminal Justice Act, 1991) requires juveniles under 18 to be separated from persons 18 or over who have been charged with criminal offences, except relatives and adults with whom they are charged (in certain circumstances). This applies to juveniles (under 18 years) detained at the police station, being conveyed to or from court or after attending court.

The Criminal Justice Act 1991 affects juveniles in other ways, namely:

- The jurisdiction of youth courts extends to 17-year-olds for trial and sentence.

- Remand hearings for 17-year-olds will likewise normally take place in the youth court, even though the court's powers in relation to them remain the same as that for adults.

- Exceptions to the general rule include:

     17-year-olds who must be brought before a court within a set time and no youth court is sitting

     17-year-olds jointly charged with persons of 18 years or over

  In which case they may be dealt with by a magistrates' court.

THE `APPROPRIATE ADULT'

Q What is an 'appropriate adult' in relation to juveniles?
A An appropriate adult can be any of the following people:

1: His parent or guardian

If in care:
- the care authority
- the voluntary organisation.

C
CODE
1.7 &
Note 1C

NOTE ONE

'In care' is used to cover cases where the juvenile is being 'looked after' by a local authority under the Children Act 1989.

NOTE TWO

The parent or guardian should be the appropriate adult unless:

- suspected of involvement in the offence
- the victim.
- a witness
- involved in the investigation
- received admissions prior to acting as the appropriate adult.

Where the parent is estranged (does not live with the juvenile), he should not be asked to be the 'appropriate adult' where the juvenile objects.

2: A social worker

NOTE

Where a child in care admits an offence to a social worker, another social worker should act as the appropriate adult (other than when the worker is acting as an appropriate adult) in the interests of fairness.

C
CODE
Note 1D

3: Failing 1 or 2 above, another responsible adult aged 18 or over who is not a police officer or employed by the police

NOTE

A solicitor cannot act as an appropriate adult unless he is the parent, relative or friend and leaves his solicitor's hat outside the door. This would also apply to lay visitors.

C
CODE
Note 1F

ARREST OF A JUVENILE

Q   What special provisions apply to the arrest of juveniles for an offence?

C
CODE
Note 11C

A i)   A juvenile should not be arrested at his place of education unless this is unavoidable and the head or his deputy must be informed.

A (ii) In addition to being liable to arrest for 'Breach of Bail Conditions', (in the same way as adults), juveniles can also be arrested for 'Breaching Conditions of Remand', ie having been refused bail and remanded into local authority accommodation with bail type conditions, has breached those conditions. (See section 23A of the C&YP Act 1969)

A (iii) The principle of only arresting and detaining persons when necessity so demands should always apply to juveniles. Whenever possible interviews should be carried out at their homes.

A bad decision by a constable to arrest and detain a juvenile is sometimes compounded by a custody officer more concerned with saving the constable any embarrassment than operating professionally.

Special Provisions

1. **Initial action** at a police station consists of the custody officer (if practicable):

C CODE 3.7

- ascertaining the identity of the person responsible for the juvenile's welfare, (which may or may not be the appropriate adult)
- as soon as practicable, informing him of arrest, why arrested, where detained, and that a decision is to be made regarding laying an information.

NOTE

In the case of a juvenile under a supervision order, reasonable steps must be taken to notify the person supervising him.

C CODE 3.8

Where a juvenile is in the care of a local authority etc but is living with his parent or other adult responsible for his welfare then (although there is no legal obligation) they too should normally be contacted (unless suspected of involvement in the offence concerned).

C CODE 3C

Even where a juvenile is not living with his parents, consideration should be given to informing them. This right is in addition to the juvenile's right to have someone informed of his detention.

2. **Rights and entitlements** apply to juveniles...

- The provision of oral and written information (see Legal Advice Formula – Chapter 2. 'Right to Legal Advice)

- The right to have someone informed of the arrest at public expense

- The right to access in person, by writing or telephone, to free, independent legal advice and subject to the same delay of rights by a superintendent, etc (except that the appropriate adult may also be involved as an advisor or decision maker – see post).

NOTE

The juvenile has a right to consult privately with a solicitor without the appropriate adult being present.

C CODE 1. EE

- The entitlement to communicate directly with one person by letter or telephone is subject to denial or delay of rights by an inspector

NOTE ONE

In relation to a juvenile who may not understand what is being said to him, if he wishes to have legal advice the appropriate action should be taken straight away. It should not be delayed until the appropriate adult arrives.

NOTE TWO

See the paragraph post regarding the role of the appropriate adult.

CUSTODY RECORD – RIGHTS/ENTITLEMENTS

Must

> Record the contact with the person responsible for the welfare of the detained juvenile
>
> Record notification to the 'supervisor' of a detained juvenile (subject of a supervision order)

Advise to record

> Any attempts or difficulties in relation to contacting either of the above
>
> Any request or offer to contact any person specified in the codes made by an agent for a care authority or voluntary organisation

---

2315   Mrs Suzanne McDougal, Social Services Department, informs me that she will contact both the 'supervising officer' and the detained person's parents in the morning of 26.9.95. The detainee resides in Rose's residential care establishment, not with his parents.

---

3. Conditions & Treatment

Q   *What special provisions apply to the condition and treatment of detained juveniles?*

A1 Cell accommodation

C
CODE
8.8

Juveniles under the age of 18 should not be placed in a cell unless no other secure accommodation is available and the custody officer considers that it is not practicable to supervise him if not placed in a cell. However where the cell is more comfortable than other secure accommodation then the cell can be used, but he must not be placed in a cell with a detained adult (ie a person 18 or over).

| C |
| CODE |
| 8.8 |

NOTE

Whenever possible juveniles (and other persons at risk) should be visited more regularly.

A2 Intimate and strip searches and samples

| C |
| CODE |
| Note 8A |

The special procedures in relation to the intimate and strip search of a juvenile detainee revolve around the 'appropriate adult' (see post for appropriate adult and Chapter 1 for full details of intimate and strip searches). (Also see Chapter 8 for intimate and non-intimate samples).

| C |
| CODE |
| Annex A |

A3 Right to a copy/inspect the custody record by the juvenile and appropriate adult. (See appropriate adult, post).

| C |
| CODE |
| 2.4 & 2.5 |

CUSTODY RECORD – DETAINED JUVENILES

Must

Record reasons why placed in a cell
Record when the juvenile and his 'appropriate adult' inspect the custody record

Advise to record

Any breaches of the requirement under PACE in relation to cell accommodation and the reason for that decision
Any use of force or restraint against such a vulnerable person together with the reasons why it was necessary

1050   The juvenile was placed in a cell because of his violent nature and the fact that the detention room for juveniles was occupied.

Force was used to put him into the cell – he jammed his legs against the cell door frame and was pushed into the cell, with no apparent injury to him or PC Smith and myself.

4. Questioning, charging, and authorisation of continued detention

C
CODE
11.14

Q What special provisions apply to the interviewing of juveniles?

A The provisions relate to the presence of an appropriate adult at the interview of a juvenile, unless the urgency is present as at Code C 11.1 and Annex C..

Q What special provisions apply to the charging and detention of juveniles?

A As above the provisions relate to the presence and actions of the appropriate adult in relation to:

C
CODE
16.1,
3 & 4

C
CODE
15.1 & 2

1 Charging
2 Statements made by another
3 Contents of an interview with another
4 Reviews of detention (inspector)
5 Authorisation of further detention (superintendent) (see appropriate adult post).

PACE
S 38

The criteria for detention after charge are the same as those for adults, ie in relation to:

- Name and address; or
- Fail to honour bail; or
- Interfere with justice; or
- Own protection; or
- Imprisonable or non-imprisonable offences.

(See Reviews Chapter 5 ante for full details).

Plus the added alternative of a reasonable belief that detention after charge is necessary for his own interest.

In practice this juvenile specific criterion will rarely be used as the adult criteria will normally cover most circumstances. That said, the word 'interest' has a wider meaning than 'own protection' (under the adult interview) and could include moral, social and educational considerations.

Having decided that the juvenile will be detained after charge the custody officer must arrange for a transfer into local authority accommodation from which the juvenile will subsequently be produced before a youth court.

C
CODE
16.6

There are only **two exceptions** whereby the juvenile need not go into local authority accommodation, pending his appearance at court, these are:

- **Not Practicable**

The Codes of Practice warn that factors such as:

C
CODE16.
6 & 16B

The Time of Day or Night
The Juvenile's Behaviour
The Nature of the Offence Charged
The Lack of Secure Accommodation

are irrelevant to the 'practicability' of transferring the juvenile into the care of the local authority. Relevant grounds could include severe weather conditions, or the difficulties in contacting social services, despite repeated attempts.

NOTE

Where it is impracticable the custody officer must record the reasons and complete a certificate to accompany the juvenile to court.

<table>
<tr><td>C
CODE
16.6</td></tr>
</table>

• **The juvenile is 12 years or above; and no 'secureaccommodation' is available; and there is a 'risk to the public of serious harm'**

NOTE ONE

Serious harm would include death, or serious bodily injury, whether physical or psychological, from further offences.

NOTE TWO

Home Office Circular No 78/1992 (Detention of Juveniles) gives strict guidance to assist the custody officer.

NOTE THREE

Another Home Office Circular (242/70) suggests the responsibility of conveying juveniles to and from court is the 'responsibility of the police'.

However, 'local arrangements' may apply in your area concerning transportation to 'secure accommodation' in youth courts. You may consider 'transferring custody' on arrival rather than 'assisting others' to transport them to avoid any complications concerning whether or not officers were in the 'lawful execution of their duty'.

NOTE FOUR

Where a juvenile is moved to the local authority as above, the custody officer's duty in relation to that juvenile to abide by the Codes and maintain a custody record, shall cease.

NOTE FIVE

When detention is outside the above criteria, ie the juvenile is not 12 years old or further offences do not render the public liable to serious harm, custody officers cannot make demands for secure accommodation. The place of detention is at the discretion of the local authority.

POINTS OF PRACTICE

Moved to local authority accommodation

The juvenile could be released on bail to the court in such circumstances. When appropriate it is suggested that he be transferred to the local authority after being unconditionally released from police detention.

There seems little point in bailing a juvenile, particularly as the agent for the local authority would probably refuse to act as a surety.

Further offence when on bail

When a juvenile is arrested and is already on bail to a court to appear in a few days' time, a custody officer may prefer not to charge the offence, but to TIC it, ie taken into consideration with the original offence.

Charging the juvenile with the second offence could result in an adjournment which would effectively put the person back 'on the streets' without punishment or otherwise. A TIC would allow the first case to proceed and also bring the youth court's attention to the admitted second offence

Juvenile and sureties

When a juvenile is bailed a surety is normally called for. The parent or guardian could stand surety. A recognisance to secure a juvenile's attendance at court could include a requirement for the attendance of the parent or guardian at court. The custody officer could consider placing the juvenile under local authority care when the parent or guardian refuses to act as a surety, though this does seem somewhat extreme.

MENTALLY DISORDERED – MENTALLY HANDICAPPED ETC

Q *What special provisions apply to the arrest, detention condition and treatment of mentally disordered or handicapped persons (who are not unlawfully at large from a hospital).*

A Much depends on the reason for the detention. There are two basic ways:

- Detention under the Mental Health Act

- Arrest for an offence

When detained under the Mental Health Act the detainee should be assessed as soon as possible

C
CODE
3.10

NOTE

The Codes of Practice advise, in cases where:

C
CODE
Annex E 5

On arrival at the police station a person appears to be suffering from a mental disorder, or is incoherent other than through drunkenness alone, **or**

A detained person subsequently appears to be mentally disordered

the custody officer must immediately:

call the police surgeon, or if urgent

send the person to hospital, or

call the most available medical practitioner.

However, it does advocate the primacy of an assessment under the Mental Health Act 1983, providing it can be done without undue delay.

If at a police station, a registered medical practitioner and an approved social worker should be called to interview and examine him.

Once examined and interviewed and suitable arrangements made for treatment and care, he should no longer be detained.

Arrest for an offence

Where the custody officer authorises detention of a person with mental problems he must inform an appropriate adult (see post) as soon as possible, explaining the reason for detention and invite the adult to attend. The detainee's rights including the caution and entitlements should be given to him in the presence of an appropriate adult; or repeated in front of the appropriate adult when he is present.

C
CODE
Annex E(3)

C
CODE
Annex E E2

This right to legal advice should not be delayed until the adult arrives, when the detainee has requested it. When an adult is called to the station the detainee should also be allowed to consult privately with a solicitor in the absence of the adult. (See also Code C 1EE).

The appropriate adult can request legal advice on behalf of the detainee (see Annex E.4).

C
CODE
Annex E(8)

The detainee should not be interviewed without the adult unless it is to prevent interference or harm etc described under C Code 11.1 and Annex C (see also Annex E, Note E4). Once the risk has been averted, questioning should stop until the adult is present. A record should be made of the reasons for any such questioning.

C
CODE
Annex E 9
& 12

The appropriate adult also has a crucial role to play in all the subsequent key PACE procedures, including interviews, reviews, charging and intimate/strip searches (see post).

NOTE

Arrest or a detention under the Mental Health Act are mutually exclusive. It is not possible to switch from one path to another.

When a person is arrested for an offence and is subsequently found to be mentally disordered or mentally handicapped it may be best practice to either:

Write off the crime under Home Office guidelines and unconditionally release him, having assisted him to obtain all necessary help, or

Charge the detainee and place before a court, either on bail or in custody, appraising the court of all the circumstances.

Continued detention

Again the necessity principle should be applied having due regard to the person's mental state. Generally, a police station is not a suitable place to detain such a person.

CUSTODY RECORD – MENTAL HEALTH

Must

Record arrangements made to contact both the registered medical practitioner and the approved social worker including their estimated time of arrival

Record any examination and instructions from either of the above professionals

Record the reasons for any interview or questions in the absence of an appropriate adult

Advise to record

Any other person contacted and information obtained, eg detainee's general practitioner, family and mental institution

Any special arrangements for the detainee's care and custody.

03.45	Dr Simpson and Mrs Dickinson both contacted and said they would attend at 0600 hours.
0600	Both above arrived and Dr Simpson examined detainee. Pronounced physically fit but suggested an immediate return to hospital. Mr Dickinson arranged his return to Notown Mental Hospital.
0700	Mrs Jones, detainee's mother informed of the circumstances.

WHEN TO TREAT AS MENTALLY DISORDERED ETC

C
CODE
1.4

*Q   When should a person be treated as mentally disordered,
mentally handicapped or mentally incapable of
understanding the significance of questions put to him?*

A   If an officer suspects or is told in good faith that a person of
any age may be mentally disturbed or, mentally incapable of
understanding the significance of questions put to him or his
replies,then he shall be dealt with as being mentally
disordered or mentally handicapped for the purpose of the
code.

(See Code C Note 1G for further description of mental
disorder).

Once again the PACE Act offers protection to the above
group of people, whom it sees as vulnerable.

It provides a guardian, similar to juveniles, in the form of the
'appropriate adult'.

Appropriate adult for mentally disturbed

C
CODE
1.7(b)

*Q   What is an 'appropriate adult' for mentally disordered and
mentally handicapped persons?*

A   • A relative

• A guardian

• A person responsible for his care or custody, someone who
has experience of dealing with mentally disordered or
mentally handicapped persons (but not a police officer or
employee), or

If none of the above is available, some other responsible adult
aged 18 or over (not a police officer or employee).

NOTE

C
CODE
Note 1E & 1F
& Annex E
(E1)

The Code prefers an experienced or trained person, but
where the detainee indicates a relative, his wishes should
if practicable, be respected.

A solicitor present at the station in his professional
capacity should not act as an appropriate adult.

Special Provisions

1: Initial action

The custody officer must (as soon as practicable) inform the appropriate adult. (See paragraph, post, regarding the role of the appropriate adult).

2: Rights and entitlements

All the normal rights and entitlements are due to mentally disturbed persons:

• The provision of oral or written information (see Legal Advice Formula, Chapter 2. 'Right to Legal Advice).

- The right to have someone informed of the arrest at public expense.

- The right to direct access in person, by writing or telephone, to free independent legal advice and subject to the same delay of rights by a superintendent.

- The entitlement to communicate directly by letter or telephone, subject to the same denial or delay of rights by an inspector.

The appropriate adult may be involved as an advisor or decision maker. (See 'appropriate adult' post).

NOTE

When the detainee wishes to have legal advice the appropriate action should be taken straight away and not delayed until the appropriate adult arrives.

C
CODE
Note 3G

3: Conditions and treatment

There are no special provisions under the codes, with the possible exception of cell visits and the use of handcuffs.

Whenever possible any persons at risk should be visited more regularly.

C
CODE
Note8A
& Annex 13

Additionally the appropriate adult should be involved in relation to:

- Intimate and strip searches

- Inspecting a copy of the custody record (see paragraph post regarding the role of the appropriate adult).

4: Questioning, charging, reviews and authorisation of continued detention

C
CODE
11.14

The appropriate adult plays an important part in the questioning of mentally disordered or mentally handicapped persons, given the possibility of unreliable evidence and the need for corroboration wherever possible (see Annex E. Note E3). He may also be involved in the procedures of:

1 Charging
2 Statements made by another
3 Contents of an interview with another
4 Reviews of detention (inspector)
5 Authorisation of continued detention (superintendent)

C
CODE
15 & 16

(See next paragraph for appropriate adult).

THE APPROPRIATE ADULT

In keeping with the spirit of the PACE Act the appropriate adult is a built-in safeguard, which, it is fair to say, many police forces were using long before 1984.

Their key role applies to juveniles and persons mentally disordered or handicapped and they have been defined at Juveniles and Mentally Disordered Persons ante.

The following should not be 'appropriate adults' even if a parent or guardian:

- the victim
- possibly involved in the offence
- a witness to the offence
- involved in the investigation
- received admissions prior to becoming an appropriate adult..

C
CODE
Note 1C &
1D

NOTE

Persons acting in the capacity of solicitors, or lay visitors, cannot fulfil a dual role and act a an appropriate adult.

If a juvenile admits an offence in front of a social worker who is not acting as an appropriate adult, another social worker should be appointed as an appropriate adult.

If the parent is estranged from a juvenile, he should not act as an appropriate adult if the juvenile objects in his presence.

NOTE

The custody officer should see the appropriate adult as an ally whose presence will facilitate reliable communications with these vulnerable groups. Admissions and confessions should be more acceptable to the courts when the appropriate adult is present.

Their involvement in the following procedures is specified in the Codes of Practice:

1: Contacting the appropriate adult

When a person requiring an appropriate adult is brought to a police station under arrest, or is arrested after attending there voluntarily, the custody officer must as soon as practicable contact the appropriate adult and inform him of:

C
CODE
3.9

- the grounds for his detention
- his whereabouts, **and**
- ask the adult to come to see the detainee.

229

CUSTODY RECORD – CONTACTING APPROPRIATE ADULT

Must

Record contact with the appropriate adult, the relationship of the adult to the detainee **and** request the adult to attend at the police station to see the detainee. Show estimated time of arrival.

Advise to record

Any attempt or difficulty in relation to contacting the appropriate adult

Any decision by the juvenile detainee to refuse to allow a particular person to act as the appropriate adult by virtue of being estranged

1720	Tried to contact the father, Mark Dickinson, but no answer to telephone 123 456 7890.
1725	Still no answer
1730	Contacted by telephone and said he would attend at 1800 hours.

2: Information – rights and entitlements

When the appropriate adult is already at the police station when information is given to the detainee as mentioned in Code C 3.1 to 3.5 then:

> The information must be given to the detained person in his presence.

C CODE 3.11

If the appropriate adult is not at the police station when the information is given then:

> The information must be given again when the adult arrives.

NOTE ONE

The notice of entitlements given to the detainee includes information about the circumstances in which an appropriate adult can assist.

C CODE Note 3A

NOTE TWO

When cautioned in the absence of the appropriate adult, a further caution should be given in the adult's presence and recorded in a pocket book or interview record.

C CODE 10.6

NOTE THREE

The detainee should be told that the appropriate adult is there to assist and advise at any time, privately or not.

C CODE 3.12

It is suggested that the right to consult privately may be instigated by the adult, as well as the detainee.

CUSTODY RECORD – INFORMATION

Must

> Record where the appropriate adult is when information is given to the detainee
> Whether the information was repeated in front of the adult
> Record that advice was given to the detainee that he could consult at any time, privately or not, with the appropriate adult

---

1830   Information given to the detainee in the presence of the father. Further, that he could talk to his father, in private or not, at any time.

3: Initiating access to legal advice

<table>
<tr><td>C
CODE
1EE &
1.1</td></tr>
</table>

It is imperative that the custody officer reminds the appropriate adult and the detainee of the right to Free Independent Legal Advice, through personal access or via the telephone, and records any reasons for waiving it. Additionally the detainee should be informed of his right to private consultation with the solicitor, without the appropriate adult.

NOTE ONE

<table>
<tr><td>C
CODE
Note 3G</td></tr>
</table>

The use of the abbreviation N/A (not applicable) in connection with appropriate adults, etc must be used with care, if it is used at all. When decisions are made under the PACE Act reasons should be shown. It is too easy to deny a person's rights or entitlements by the use of N/A. To deny such matters may lead to the exclusion of vital evidence by the court.

NOTE TWO

<table>
<tr><td>C
CODE
6.4</td></tr>
</table>

When the detainee wishes to have legal advice the appropriate action should be taken immediately and not delayed until the appropriate adult arrives.

No attempt should be made to dissuade the detainee from obtaining legal advice.

NOTE THREE

<table>
<tr><td>C
CODE
3.13</td></tr>
</table>

Once the detainee or the appropriate adult decides that legal advice should be taken then Code C paragraph 6 applies, (See Chapter 2).

232

CUSTODY RECORD – INITIATING ACCESS TO LEGAL ADVICE

Must

Record when the appropriate adult is present when a detainee requests legal advice. (The adult should countersign the detainee's signature)

Record the action taken when the appropriate adult determines that the detainee needs legal advice, either at the time when the detainee is informed or subsequently

2005　The detainee requested legal advice and Mrs Helen Bainbridge contacted and will attend at 2100 hours today.

4: Interviews – Statements under caution

It is important to note that juveniles and mentally disordered or handicapped persons may, without realising or wishing to do so, provide information which is unreliable, misleading or self-incriminating.

C CODE Note 11B

Special care should be taken in questioning such people and the appropriate adult should be called upon where doubt exists re the person's age, mental state or capacity.

Because of this risk corroboration is necessary whenever possible of any fact admitted.

The custody officer is not directly involved in the above but he plays a vital role with the information and briefing to the appropriate adult.

Interviews

A juvenile or a person who is mentally disturbed, whether suspected or not, must not be interviewed without an appropriate adult unless Annex C or C Code 11.1 applies, ie an urgent interview needed to prevent immediate risk of:

C CODE 11.14

- interfere/harm to persons or evidence or
- hinder property recovery from an offence, or
- alerting other suspects

C
CODE
11.16

Where the appropriate adult is present at an interview he should be informed:

- That he is not simply an observer

- That he is there to advise the detained person

- That he should observe whether the interview is proper and fair

- That he should facilitate communication with the person.

NOTE

The custody officer should advise the officer in the case of the appropriate adult's role.

There is a danger when the appropriate adult threatens the interviewee or is oppressive in some other way. The courts could well exclude the resulting evidence.

A good interviewer always assesses the attitude of the appropriate adult before the interview and advises him accordingly. Parents are generally upset by their offspring's actions and tend to shout or threaten during the interview. They should be warned that such outbursts could ruin the fairness of the interview. If necessary, the interview should be paused and the parent warned about him conduct whilst the tape is running.

An example of the above:

Where a parent told his son during an interview, 'Tell the truth or you won't go home unless you do', the court excluded the confessions that followed.

NOTE

The appropriate adult may also interrupt the detainee's 8 hour period of rest, free from questioning, etc, without prejudice to PACE.

C
CODE
12.2

Statements under caution

As with interviews above, a juvenile or mentally disordered or mentally handicapped person must not be asked to provide or sign a written statement in the absence of the appropriate adult, (unless Annex C or Code C 11.1 applies).

C
CODE
11.14

Annex D of Code C deals with written statements under caution, ie written by the person under caution, or written by a police officer.

CUSTODY RECORD – INTERVIEWS AND STATEMENTS UNDER CAUTION

Must

Record the names of all those present at the interview including the appropriate adult

NOTE

When the appropriate adult or the solicitor is present during the interview he should be given the opportunity to read and sign the interview record (or any written statement taken by a police officer)

C
CODE
11.11

Advise to record

Any comments made outside the interview, if relevant to the offence, etc. He should be asked to endorse the record with the words 'I agree that this is a correct record of what was said' and sign it

C
CODE
11.13 &
11D

The appropriate adult should also be given the opportunity to read and sign them

---

Example

1515   The detainee was interviewed and the following
persons were present:

    1   detainee

    2   PC Clare Girdwood (interviewing officer)

    3   Mrs Tracy Small (solicitor)

    4   Mr John Logan (detainee's father and appropriate
adult)

5: Reviews

Review by inspector

An opportunity should be provided for the appropriate adult to
make representations.

NOTE

C
CODE
15.1

The Code uses the words 'if available at the time'.
Normally the appropriate adult will have left the police
station. Good practice would dictate advising the
appropriate adult of the procedure and allowing him to
make early representations, which can be recorded for
the benefit of the review officer who will conduct the
next review.

Review by superintendent

C
CODE
15.2

A similar opportunity should be given under the superintendent
or above's review for an authorisation for continued detention.

CUSTODY RECORD – REVIEWS

Advise to record

The opportunity given to the appropriate adult and any
representations as to:

the review of detention, or

an authority for further detention

6: Charging of detained persons
Charging

i)   When an officer considers there is sufficient evidence for a prosecution to succeed,

C
CODE
16.1

ii) That the detainee has said all he wishes to say about the offence,

iii) He should without delay bring him before the custody officer,

- Who is responsible for considering whether he should be charged.

- Where detained for more than one offence no need to bring before the custody officer until i) and ii) are satisfied for all the offences.

Any resulting action should take place in the presence of the appropriate adult when a juvenile or mentally disordered or mentally handicapped person is involved.

NOTE

The input of the appropriate adult can be very useful to the custody officer at this stage, especially when the appropriate adult is from another agency and able to offer alternatives to charging such as intermediate treatment following a caution, or voluntary attendance at a mental institution.

These alternatives could prove to be quite attractive when valuable police and court resources are taken into account. The paramount objective is that of the best course for the detainee.

Written notice

C CODE 16.3

At the time of charging, the detainee shall be given a written notice showing the offence charged and other matters.

If the person is a juvenile or is mentally disordered or mentally handicapped the notice shall be given to the appropriate adult.

NOTE

C CODE 16.4

If at any time after charge or told he may be prosecuted for an offence, a police officer wishes to bring to the notice of:

- A mentally disordered or a mentally handicapped person or

- A juvenile

Any written statement made by another person, or the content of an interview with another person,

He shall give a copy of the statement or account of the interview to the appropriate adult (as well as to the detainee).

CUSTODY RECORD – CHARGING

C CODE 16.8

Must

Record any questions put after charge and answers contemporaneously on the forms provided and signed by that person or, if he refuses, by the interviewing officer and any third parties present.

Advise to record

The handing to the appropriate adult of the 'notice of charge' against signature

When a copy statement or an interview record from another person is brought to the attention of the appropriate adult

Example

14.10   When Jane Lloyd was charged with the offence, her mother, Pam Lloyd (the appropriate adult) was handed a 'notice of charge'.

Received a notice of charge.....P Lloyd.

17.10   An interview record of Michael Chew, concerning the ill treatment of goats, contrary to the Protection of Animals Act was brought to the attention of Jane Lloyd and her mother Pam Lloyd. The replies were recorded on the original interview record of Jane Lloyd by the interviewing officer, PC Neil Smith.

7: Interpreters

For the appropriate adult

An interpreter should be called if a juvenile is interviewed and the appropriate adult appears:

C CODE 13.6

- Deaf, or
- There is doubt about his hearing, or
- Speaking ability, unless
- He agrees in writing that the interview can go ahead without one, or Annex C or 11.1 of Code C applies, ie urgent interviews to prevent or mitigate harm or loss.

Authority for a police officer to act as interpreter

where there is difficulty communicating with a solicitor because of language, hearing or speech problems.

If an appropriate adult or the detained person agrees in writing, (or the interview is tape recorded under the codes), a police officer may act as an interpreter. However where legal advice is sought an 'independent' interpreter will be required. See 'Language Line' in Chapter 4 ante.

C CODE 13.9

CUSTODY RECORD – INTERPRETERS

Must

Record any action to call an interpreter under this section and any agreement to be interviewed in the absence of an interpreter

Advise to record

The provision of interpreter for deaf or speech handicapped appropriate adult and when a police officer acts as interpreter

18.05	Interpreter called and estimated time of arrival of 1830 hours (Mr Thomas James Smith of Moss Side).
18.45	Contacted Mr Smith's residence and informed that he had been diverted elsewhere and can't attend.
18.50	Detainee agreed to be interviewed without an independent interpreter. PC Patel to interpret at taped interview Signed Neville Newton (Detainee)

8: Inspection – Copy of the custody record

C CODE 2.4

When an appropriate adult first arrives at the police station he is entitled to read the detainee's custody records. Further when a person leaves police detention or is taken before a court, the appropriate adult can have a copy of the custody record as soon as practicable. This entitlement lasts for 12 months after release.

C CODE 2.5

When the appropriate adult gives reasonable notice of a request to inspect the original custody record (after the detainee has left police detention) he should be allowed to do so.

CUSTODY RECORD – INSPECTION OF CUSTODY RECORD

Must

Record any inspection of the original custody record by the appropriate adult etc after the detainee has left police detention

Advise to record

When a copy of the custody record is supplied to a juvenile etc or appropriate adult

9: Evidence Gathering Procedures

Where any detainee is a juvenile or a person who is mentally disordered or mentally handicapped then any procedure requiring that that person be given specific information, requiring the detainee's consent, or requiring their participation, then the presence of an appropriate adult and, where applicable, his consent, is an essential requirement. These relevant specialist procedures involving the 'Appropriate Adult' are shown below.

Procedure	Consent	Information to be given	Presence Allowed	Note
Intimate & Strip Searches			(C - Annex B)	Juvenile* Proviso
Fingerprints	Where appropriate (D - 3.1)	Speculative search (D - 3.2A)	Destruction (D - 3.4)	
Photographs	Where appropriate (D - 4.1)		Destruction (D - 4.4)	
Intimate Samples	Where appropriate (D - 5.1)	Speculative search (D - 5.11A) Grounds and Offence (D - 5.11B) Legal Advice and Warning (D - 5.2 & 5A)	Removal of Clothing (D - 5.12)	Juvenile* Proviso
Non-Intimate Samples	Where appropriate (D - 5.4)	Speculative Search (D - 5.11A) Grounds and Offence (D - 5.11B)	Removal of Clothing (D - 5.12)	Juvenile* Proviso

NB* Juvenile Proviso – Juveniles have the right to request the appropriate adult to leave, providing they signify this in writing.

10: Persons blind, visually handicapped or unable to read

> C CODE 3.14

The appropriate adult (solicitor, relative or some other interested person not involved in the investigation) should be made available by the custody officer to help in checking any documentation.

Where the Code requires written consent or signification then the appropriate adult etc may be asked to sign if the detained person so wishes. This should protect both the suspect and the police.

PERSONS DEAF, BLIND, VISUALLY HANDICAPPED OR UNABLE TO READ

1: Deaf, or doubt about hearing or speaking ability or ability to understand English

> C CODE 3.6

In these cases when the custody officer cannot establish effective communication, the custody officer must:
- As soon as possible
- Call an interpreter and
- Ask him to explain his rights and entitlements.

> C CODE 13.5 & 13.6

Again where the detainee appears to fall within one of the above cases an interpreter should be called before being interviewed. When an appropriate adult acts for his juvenile offspring (including a guardian) and he appears to fall within the above cases, an interpreter should be called.

NOTE

Unless, in either case, he agrees in writing, (or Annex C or Code C 11.1 applies see post).

> C CODE 13.7

Where an interpreter is used in these circumstances he should be given the opportunity to read the record of interview and to certify its accuracy in case he is called to give evidence.

> C CODE Note 3D

Most local authority social services departments have a list of interpreters for the deaf.

The local community relations council may have a list for those who do not understand English. Most force operation rooms keep up-to-date interpreter lists.

NOTE

Under Annex C of Code C, 1(c) a person who has difficulty understanding English or who has a hearing disability may be interviewed in the absence of an interpreter for urgent interview to prevent or minimise harm or loss (described under Code C 11.1).

2: Blind or seriously visually handicapped or is unable to read

The custody officer should ensure that:

- his solicitor
- his relative
- the appropriate adult, or
- some other person likely to take an interest in him (and not involved in the investigation)

is available to help in checking any documentation.

C
CODE
3.14

Where the code requires any written consent etc, the custody officer may ask the person assisting to sign, if the detainee so wishes, as he may be unwilling to sign himself.

C
CODE
3 F

Under Annex D of Code C, if the person making a statement cannot read (or refuses) the senior police officer present shall read it to him, ask him to correct, alter or add anything and to put his signature or make his mark at the end. The police officer should certify on the statement what has occurred.

CUSTODY RECORD – BLIND, DEAF ETC

Must

Record any arrangements made to assist the detainee to check any documentation

Record the reason why the person assisting the detainee signs any consent etc instead of the detainee

A check with the force standing orders is also essential

ILLEGAL IMMIGRANTS AND FOREIGN NATIONALS

The above persons come to police notice as suspected of being:

- Illegal immigrants/entrants
- Overstaying their permitted time
- Subject of a deportation order, or
- Working in breach of visa conditions.
- Guilty of an offence

Such people can be held under the administrative powers of the Immigration Acts, or the criminal or common law powers of arrest..

1: Illegal immigrants

| C CODE 1.10 |

The PACE Act applies to detainees held under the Immigration Acts (except that Part IV of PACE Act (Detention) does not apply to person temporarily detained on an order made by an immigration officer, prior to deportation).

The Codes do not apply to:

| C CODE 1.12 |

- Persons arrested for fingerprinting under section.3(5) Asylum and Immigration Appeals Act 1993 or

- those served with a notice for detention under the Immigration Act 1971 but minimum standards of detention under Code C 8 and 9 ante, apply.

The Codes of Practice apply to any person in police detention. Where held under administrative powers (not an offence) the Immigration office should be consulted prior to actioning prisoner's rights and entitlements.

2: Foreign nationals

A citizen of an independent Commonwealth country or a national of a foreign country (including the Republic of Ireland) may communicate at any time with his:

C
CODE
7.1

- High Commission
- Embassy or
- Consulate.

He must be told that he can have one of the above informed:

- Of his whereabouts and
- The grounds for his detention.

These rights must be communicated to him and any request acted upon as soon as practicable. They should be included in the written notice under Code C note 3A.

Other languages, such as Welsh, the main minority groups and EC countries should be kept where necessary.

Consular convention

If the detainee's country has a bilateral consular convention in force requiring notification of arrest (see full list in Code C Annex F as at 1.1.95) the appropriate High Commission, Embassy or Consulate shall be informed as soon as practicable, except:

C
CODE
7.2

When the detainee is a:

- Political refugee (whether for reasons of race, nationality, political opinion or religion) or is seeking

C
CODE
7.4

- political asylum

the consulate shall not be

- informed of the arrest
- given access to, or
- given information about him

unless at the detainee's express request.

NOTE

C CODE 7.3

Consular officials may visit one of their nationals to talk to him and if necessary arrange legal advice.

Such visits should be outside the hearing of the police.

Depending on the circumstances of each case the custody officer or officer dealing should involve the local immigration office and other interested parties such as Customs and Excise officers.

C CODE 7A

The rights outlined above should not be interfered with even though Code C Annex B applies (urgent interviews).

CUSTODY RECORD – FOREIGN NATIONALS ETC

Must

Record when the detainee is informed of his rights

Record any communication with a High Commission, Embassy or Consulate

21.30 The detainee Robert Lloyd (a French national) informed of his right to

- communicate with his High Commission etc
- have them informed of his whereabouts and reason for detention.

21.47 The French Embassy official, Ian Ewee, informed of the whereabouts of Robert Lloyd and the fact that he has been arrested for landing 6 illegal Turkish immigrants in his yacht, 'Pompanette'.

WARDS OF COURT

Certain minors are made wards of court under an order made by the High Court.

This does not apply to a child who is subject of a care order.

Such a wardship imposes certain restrictions on the procedures contained in the PACE Act:

i) The wardship court should be informed of the arrest and detention of the ward of court.

ii) The leave of the court should be obtained prior to questioning the ward (except in cases requiring immediate actions, eg serious offences against the ward, or where the ward is suspected of committing an offence).

In Re R and G (Minors) [1990] FCR 495 it was held that if the police wish to interview a suspect, or a victim who is a ward of court and there is no time to seek the leave of the court, the police will have no extra duty other than to comply with the requirements of the PACE Act.

Those having the care of the minor must inform the court at the earliest practical opportunity of what has happened.

iii) The consent of the court should be obtained prior to the taking of intimate samples.

iv) Action should not be taken against the ward without leave of the court.

Chapter 8

SPECIAL PROCEDURES

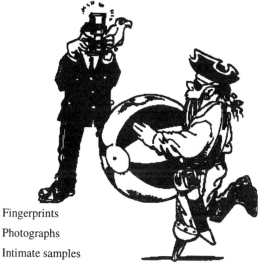

Fingerprints

Photographs

Intimate samples

Non-intimate samples

Identification

Death of person in police custody

Lay visitors

Breach of the peace

Breach of bail conditions

Drug searches

Domestic violence

Most of the above subjects are not strictly the province of the custody officer. Many have specialists who are trained to deal with the finer points of these areas. However, as the custody officer has a pivotal role in the procedures, many officers seek his advice and this chapter provides the level of knowledge which the custody officer will require.

FINGERPRINTS

*Q   What authority exists to take a person's fingerprints
(including palm prints)?*

A   There are only four authorised ways in which fingerprints
(which includes palm prints) may be taken.

(1) With the person's written consent*

(2) With a superintendent's authority*

(3) After charge or report for a recordable offence*

(4) After conviction for a recordable offence*

* These also apply to taking a person's photograph.

NOTE

D CODE 3.2A	Where fingerprints are taken with or without consent, he should be informed, beforehand, that a speculative search (as defined in Code D, note 3B) may be made on them. The giving of this information should itself be recorded.

1: Written consent

When a person is at the police station at the time the consent is
given:

PACE S 61 (2) 61 (7) & (8)	(a) He must be informed - of the reason for the request - that they will be destroyed as soon as practicable, providing the conditions set out in Code D 3.4 apply (see destruction of fingerprints post).
D CODE 3.1	(b) The consent must be given in writing.

CUSTODY RECORD – FINGERPRINTS: CONSENT

Must record

I.......consent to my fingerprints (and/or photograph) being taken whilst at the police station. I have been informed that if no action is taken, or I am found not guilty they will be destroyed and I may witness this. I have also been told the reasons for taking them and that a speculative search against other prints may be made.

Signed................

Date....................

Fingerprints (and/or photographs) taken by PC57 Lawrence.

NOTE

Generally identification by fingerprints with consent is linked with identification by photographs. The two procedures are usually completed in tandem. (See post).

If not at a police station, consent could be oral.

2: Superintendent's authority

A superintendent or above may only give authorisation if (for those **not consenting,** aged over 10 years of age and detained at police station) he has reasonable grounds:

(i) for suspecting the person has been involved in a crime AND

(ii) for believing that the fingerprints will tend to confirm or disprove his involvement.

PACE
S 61 (3)
to (5)

NOTE ONE

This authority can only be given if he has not previously given his fingerprints for this offence.

NOTE TWO

Authorisation can be given orally or in writing. If given orally, it must be confirmed in writing as soon as practicable.

NOTE THREE

D
CODE
3.1

He must be informed:

- of the reason for the request
- that they will be destroyed as soon as practicable, providing the conditions set out in Code D 3.4 apply (see destruction of fingerprints).

NOTE FOUR

D
CODE
3.2

Reasonable force may be used to take authorised fingerprints.

In practice it is very difficult to take a person's fingerprints forcibly. The persons cooperation should always be sought and if necessary time should be made available for him to accept the idea or come to terms with it. Any legal adviser may help to obtain the necessary cooperation.

**CUSTODY RECORD –
FINGERPRINTS: WITHOUT CONSENT**

Must record

as soon as possible the reason for taking fingerprints **without** consent and their destruction
when force is used, the circumstances and those present

1145 hrs   Superintendent Calligan has authorised that the person's fingerprints be taken because he has reasonable grounds for suspecting his involvement in the offence of theft and for believing that his fingerprint will tend to confirm or disprove his involvement. That is, by a fingerprint being found on a bottle at the scene of the theft and the prisoner denies being inside the premises.

The prisoner has been informed of the reason for the taking of his fingerprints and the procedures for witnessing the destruction.

Signed P Harper Custody Sergeant.

NOTE

Care should now be taken as to when the evidence should be introduced at an interview with the detainee.

3: Charged or reported

Fingerprints may be taken **without consent** from a person aged over ten years detained at a police station if:

PACE
S 61 (3)

(i) He has been charged or informed he will be reported for a recordable offence.

NOTE

A recordable offence is one of those offences for which convictions are recorded in national police records. Generally, most criminal offences fall into this category, ie burglary, theft, damage etc though there are some less than obvious exceptions.

D
CODE
3A

AND

(ii) He has not had his fingerprints taken in the course of the investigation.

NOTE

He must be informed:

- of the reason for the request

- that they will be destroyed as soon as practicable, providing the conditions set out in Code D 3.4 apply (see destruction of fingerprints)

- reasonable force can be used.

4. On conviction

PACE
S 61 (6)
& 27 (1)

A person (over the age of ten years) may be fingerprinted **without consent**:

(i) if he has been convicted of a recordable offence, and

(ii) he has not been in police detention for the offence, and

(iii) he has not had his fingerprints taken

- in the course of the investigation, or

- since the conviction.

NOTE ONE

Within these provisions a person convicted of a recordable offence can be required by a constable to attend a police station to have his fingerprints taken:

- not later than a month after conviction
- within a period of seven days and
- may direct a specified time or between specified times of day.

Such attendance would not involve an arrest or the opening of a custody record.

PACE
S 27(3)

NOTE TWO

Where a person fails to attend at the police station to allow his fingerprints to be taken, he may be arrested. Reasonable force may be used to take the fingerprints.

All these matters involve the custody officer.

Also see the Immigration Act and the terrorism provisions where fingerprints may be taken.

PACE
S 64

DESTRUCTION – FINGERPRINTS

Q What must you tell a person regarding the destruction of his fingerprints?

A   He must be informed:

i) That they will be destroyed as soon as practicable provided that:

D
CODE
3.1, 3.4
& 3.5

- he is cleared of the offence
- he is not prosecuted (unless he is cautioned for it).

ii) He may witness the destruction if:

- he asks within 5 days of:
  being cleared, or
  told he will not be prosecuted.

NOTE ONE

Similar provisions exist in relation to photographs (see post).

NOTE TWO

Nothing in the above affects powers contained in the immigration and terrorism legislation (see PACE section 61, but see Code D 1.16).

PHOTOGRAPHS

Q   What authority exists for taking a person's photograph?
A   There are only five ways in which a person can be photographed:

> D
> CODE
> 4. 1-2

(1) with the person's written consent*

(2) when the person is arrested as part of a multiple arrest.

(3) after charge or report for a recordable offence.*

(4) after conviction for a recordable offence.*

(5) superintendent's authority.

*These also apply to the taking of a person's fingerprints.

These five will now be examined further.

1. Consent

<table>
<tr><td>D
CODE
4. 1</td></tr>
</table>

The provisions for taking a person's photograph with consent are identical to those for taking a person's fingerprints (see fingerprints ante). Additionally, he should be told that any significant alteration of his appearance from taking the photograph to any attempt to hold an identification procedure may be given in evidence.

2. Multiple arrests

A person's photograph may be taken without consent if:

He has been arrested at the same time as other persons, or

It is likely that other persons will be arrested and a photograph is necessary to establish:

D
CODE
4.-2

Who was arrested

The time of arrest

The place of arrest.

3. Photographed after charge or report

A person's photograph may be taken without his consent if he has been charged or reported for a recordable offence but not:

D
CODE
4.2

* released, or
* brought before a court.

NOTE

See 'Charge and Report' regarding fingerprints ante, for the definition of 'recordable offence'.

4. On conviction for a recordable offence

A person's photograph may be taken without consent if:

* He is convicted of a recordable offence, and
* His photograph is not already on record as a result of:
  * a multiple arrest for the offence, or
  * having been charged with or reported for the offence.

D
CODE
4.2

NOTE

There is no power to arrest to take a photograph after conviction. Where an arrest is necessary a power exists under section.27 PACE for fingerprinting purposes. A photograph can then be taken at the same time.

5. Superintendents authority

An arrested person's photograph may be taken where a superintendent has reasonable grounds to suspect

* involvement in a crime and
* identification evidence exists relating to the crime.

Force to photograph?

Q *Can force be used to take a person's photograph in the same way as fingerprints?*

A Under no circumstances can force be used to compel a person to have his photograph taken.

D
CODE
4.3

Destruction: photographs

Q *What must a person be told regarding the destruction of his photograph?*

A The information given to a person in relation to the destruction of his photographs is virtually identical to that for fingerprints, with the added proviso concerning previous convictions.

D
CODE
4.4

257

(Except that he may be given a certificate as evidence of destruction, instead of witnessing it, if he so requests within 5 days of being cleared or told he will not be prosecuted.)

CUSTODY RECORD – PHOTOGRAPHS		
Must		
	Record the reason why a photograph was taken without consent	
	Record when the photograph(s) are destroyed	
1115	23 May	Photographed without consent on arrival at the police office after mass arrest at large disturbance outside Sometown Football Club.
1230	20 July	Photographs and negatives shredded and a certificate completed and posted to the acquitted person at his request.

INTIMATE SAMPLES

Introduction

An intimate sample may be taken when a superintendent or above suspects that a person is involved in a recordable offence (broadly, those punishable by imprisonment).

The person's consent is required and if refused adverse inferences may be drawn by the court.

Q   What is an intimate sample?
A   A sample of: a swab taken from body orifice, (other than the mouth), urine, pubic hair, dental impression, semen, blood, or other tissue fluid.

PACE
S 65

Criteria

Q   When can intimate samples be taken from a person in police detention?
A   Only:

PACE
S 62 (1)
& (2)

• where a superintendent or above considers it will tend to confirm or disprove the suspect's involvement in a recordable offence,

D
CODE
5.1

AND

• with the suspect's written consent.

NOTE
The superintendent or above can give oral or written authorisation. If oral it must be confirmed in writing as soon as practicable.

PACE
S 63 (3)

Information to suspect

Q What information must be given to the person regarding intimate samples?

D
CODE
5.2

A Before a person is asked to provide an intimate sample he must be:

• **Reminded** (unless legally represented) of his right to free, independent legal advice using the legal formula [see Chapter 2 – 'Right to Legal Advice'] This reminder must be recorded in the custody record.

• **Warned** that a referral may harm any future case, using the words:

D
CODE
5.2 &
Note 5A

'You do not have to [provide the sample] [allow the swab or impression to be taken], but I must warn you if you refuse without good cause, your refusal may harm your case if it comes to trial.'

D
CODE
5.11A

• **Informed** that the sample may be the subject of a speculative search [see Code D and Note 5D].

D
CODE
5.11B

• **Informed** of the authorisation details:
    the grounds for the authority and the nature of the suspected offence. It is considered that a short description will suffice.

Nothing of the above affects samples taken under the immigration and terrorism legislation. [Note PACE section 62(1) to (11) applies to terrorist offences, but see Code D 1.16].

Who may take?

Q Who may take an intimate sample?

D
CODE
5.3

A Except for urine, all other intimate samples must be taken by a registered medical or dental practitioner.

NOTE ONE

We advise that you always ascertain the level of experience of the doctor or dentist in relation to preparing forensic samples.

Consider co-opting a scenes of crime officer to assist with the labelling and packaging of such samples. Care should always be taken in the custody suite regarding the cross-contamination of evidence.

Any procedure under sections 4 to 11 of the Road Traffic Act 1988 (drink driving etc) is outside this section and does not require a superintendent's authority.

PACE
S 62 (11)

Who may be present?

Q Who may be present when the intimate sample is taken?

A Where clothing needs to be removed in circumstances likely to cause embarrassment, no person of the opposite sex or whose presence is unnecessary shall be present, except a medical practitioner, a nurse; or when a juvenile requests the presence of an adult of the opposite sex who is readily available.

D
CODE
5.12

NOTE ONE

In the case of a juvenile, where he signifies in front of the appropriate adult that he would prefer the removal of clothing in the adult's absence, and the adult agrees.

D
CODE
5.12

NOTE TWO

Remember that this procedure can only be undertaken with consent so the question of force should never arise.

CUSTODY RECORD – INTIMATE SAMPLES

Must

Record the right to free, independent legal advice
Record the warning that any refusal may harm any future case
Record the information given as to a speculative search
Record as soon as practicable after the sample was taken:
    the authorisation
    grounds for authorisation
    that consent was given.
Record when written consent is given

Advise to record

    The offence for which authorised
    The person taking the sample
    The place the sample was taken
    The persons present at the taking
    The actual intimate sample taken and time taken

Example

14.55   Superintendent Griffin authorised taking the sample for the recordable offence of assault occasioning actual bodily harm on the grounds that the victim described the prisoner. A blood sample would tend to show involvement or otherwise as the attacker's blood was found on the victim. Signed D Griffin

15.00   Superintendent Griffin reminded the suspect of his right to free legal advice and his access to such advice by telephone. The suspect waived his right to legal advice, stating that he had earlier received legal advice from his solicitor Mr Brian Skelton and had been told to fully cooperate in giving intimate samples in his own best interest.(NB Recorded verbatim). He therefore felt no further need of legal advice on this subject. Superintendent Griffin also informed the suspect that any sample given may be the subject of a speculative search and warned the suspect as follows:

'You do not have to provide this sample, but I must warn you that if you refuse without good cause, your referral may harm your case if it comes to trial.'

15.05   I . . . . . . consent to provide an intimate sample of blood. Signed . . . . Detainee.

NON-INTIMATE SAMPLES

Introduction

A non-intimate sample can be taken from someone in police detention charged with or convicted of a recordable offence, without their consent. The sample does not need to be relevant to the investigation of any particular offence.

PACE
S 65

Q What exactly is a non-intimate sample?
A   Hair other than pubic hair (hair can be plucked with the root for DNA test etc) and the suspect can make a reasonable choice from where the hair is taken.

D
CODE
5.11 & Note
5C

A sample taken from a nail or under a nail

A swab from any part of the body including the mouth (but not any other body orifice.)

A specimen of saliva

A footprint or similar impression of a person's body (other than of his hand).

Criteria

*Q   When can a non-intimate sample be taken from a person in
     police detention?*
A   Either with consent or without consent.

1: With consent

> D
> CODE
> 5.4

Any consent to the taking of a non-intimate sample must be given
in writing.

2: Without consent

A non-intimate sample can only be taken without consent if:

PACE
S 63 (3)
& (4)

(i) Superintendent or above has reasonable grounds to believe a
    recordable offence involved **and** sample will tend to confirm
    or disprove the prisoner's involvement.

> D
> CODE
> 5.5

NOTE

The superintendent or above can give oral or written
authorisation. If oral it must be confirmed in writing as
soon as practicable.

PACE
S63.(5)

(ii) He is charged or reported with a recordable offence and has
     not had a sample taken or has had an unsuitable sample taken
     during the investigation.

(iii) He is convicted of a recordable offence after Code C comes
      into effect. Sections 63A PACE describes how a constable
      can require the person to attend a police station to provide a
      sample.

Information to be given

Q   What information needs to be given to the person concerned?
A   He must be given information regarding:

> D
> CODE
> 5.11A & B

i)   The fact that authorisation has been given,

ii) the grounds for giving it ,

iii) the nature of the offence.

iv) that a speculative search may be made.

Nothing of the above affects powers contained in the immigration and terrorism legislation.(Note PACE section 62(1) to (11) applies to terrorists but see Code D 1.16)

Force: non-intimate sample

Q Can force be used to take a non-intimate sample from a person who does not consent.

A Reasonable force can be used to take non-intimate samples if necessary.

D CODE 5.6

Who may be present?

Q Who may be present when the non-intimate sample is taken?

A This is the same as for intimate samples (See ante).

D CODE 5.12

NOTE

On occasions the custody staff are requested to take non-intimate samples. It is advised that whenever possible a scenes of crime officer should be asked to take the samples.

Procedures and equipment change quickly and forensic evidence is of such importance that a mistake could be very costly.

For out-of-hours emergencies it may be advisable to obtain a copy of the scenes of crime instruction manual. This could well be supplemented by telephone advice where possible.

PACE
S63 (9)

CUSTODY RECORD – NON-INTIMATE SAMPLES

Must

Record the information given as to a speculative search

Record authorisation for taking

Record the grounds for the authorisation

Record any reasonable force used and any persons present

Advise to record

Person authorising

The offence concerned

The person taking the sample

Person present at the taking

The actual non-intimate sample(s) taken

IDENTIFICATION

Identification is a growth area, with increased parades, confrontation by witnesses, showing photographs, groups and video identification. Correspondingly there are more legal challenges and more critical comment by the courts.

When the suspect is 'known', the formal identification procedures must be supervised by an 'identification officer'.

The identification officer must be an inspector or above, in uniform and not involved with the investigation. The custody officer should not be involved in these procedures, which are detailed in Code D and its appendices.

Dangers lie where police witnesses conduct their own informal confrontations and compromise the quality of such identification evidence.

Officers have in the past called at the custody suite to identify a suspect or refresh their memory as to clothing and descriptive details. Sometimes two officers will ask to look at the suspect or photographs of the suspect or discuss identification matters of a known suspect, ie a person eligible to claim his right to stand on an identification parade. The conduct of such officers would be an evidential disaster. Code D has a final warning:

> Except for the provisions of Annex D paragraph 1 (the showing of photographs) a police witness for the purposes of this part of the Code is subject to the same principles and procedures as a civilian witness.

D
CODE
Note 2A

The procedures for viewing photographs are set out in Annex D of Code D. In cases of public order and multiple arrests the use of an instant camera can be a great advantage for recording faces, clothing, injuries etc. Once again some officers involved with the case have collectively viewed photographs and have totally compromised the identity evidence.

Code D warns of the dangers of officers viewing photographs informally (see Code D. Note 4A).

DEATH IN POLICE CUSTODY

1   Anyone involved with a death in police custody will find that it is a most unpleasant experience that will never be forgotten.

2   The custody officer should be aware of the effect on his staff and consider any necessary counselling or a change of duty etc.

3   Other prisoners will be affected in negative ways and the generally good relations could be lost for a time.

4   The custody suite is potentially a crime scene and forensic evidence may need preserving. All records could be required for evidence or be requested by the coroner.

5   All custody staff actions may well be subjected to trial by hindsight.

6   Prevention is better than cure, but it is impossible to prevent certain illnesses, suicides etc.

> Knowledge of the detainee is the best preventive tool.

> Search cell block before lodging prisoner to ensure no weapons etc exist.

> Hanging, injuries and overdosing are areas to watch to prevent death in custody.

Criteria

Q   What constitutes a death in police custody?
A   When a police officer:

> arrests a person, or

> a suspect agrees to help the police enquiry without arrest, or

> a person detained or taken into custody for searching, or for his own protection

all the above will be regarded as deaths in custody whether at a police station, hospital, police car or in the street etc.

A witness dying at a police station would be included.

Not included would be persons who have left police custody whether or not on bail.

Role of custody officer

Q   What is the role of the custody officer for a death in custody?
A   Treat as a crime scene for murder:

i)   check for signs of life – call medical assistance

ii) protect the scene

iii) ensure all prisoners are secure

iv) inform the duty inspector

v) identify and retain all possible witnesses, those involved, property etc

vi) make arrangements for taking the whole cell block out of use (depending on size and layout, etc)

vii) ascertain cause of death and act on information received and any advice from coroner

viii) make notes of all events before and after death whilst fresh in the mind

ix) ensure someone completes a 'Death in Custody' form as soon as possible or at least within 48 hours – see force standing orders.

LAY VISITORS

Lay visitors observe, comment and report on:

Persons detained at police stations

Rules governing their welfare for securing a greater public understanding and confidence in this area.

Responsibility

1   The custody officer is normally responsible for lay visitors. The lay visitors' training makes them aware that their visits impose additional workload on the custody officer and to avoid shift changeover periods.

Access

2   Visitors should be allowed in the custody area immediately unless to do so would expose them to danger. Any delay should be fully explained to them.

3   They should have access to all parts of the custody suite. They will be interested in repair, decor, cleanliness, availability of blankets etc, heating, ventilation, cell bells and toilets etc.

4   They should not visit operational parts of the station such as CID or communication rooms.

5   The custody officer or one of his staff should accompany the visitors. A formal, but helpful stance is suggested.

When questioned, a group of lay visitors said that their general impression of the police was one of 'feeling abandoned', 'out in the cold' and of 'being in the way'.

6   It is suggested that the police should be seen to go out of their way to be helpful, ie to explain where necessary and to help unravel the mysterious police bureaucracy.

Access to detainees

7   Visitors should have access to any detained person including those remanded and sentenced and kept in magistrates' court cells. (Not those awaiting court appearance).

8   The detainee has the right not to see or answer visitors' questions. The escorting officer is advised to ask the detainee within the hearing of the visitors, but out of their sight, relevant questions such as:

●   Do you wish to be seen by a lay visitor?

- Have you any objections to them examining your custody record?

The detainee's permission should be sought to allow examination of his custody record. A verbal agreement would suffice.

Drunk

9 If the detainee is drunk or for some other reason is unable to permit access, the escorting officer should allow access unless it would be unsafe. If considered unsafe, verbal access through the cell door flap could take place. Where a detainee is comatose, access could be allowed for the visitors to satisfy themselves of his well-being.

Sleeping

10 Sleeping detainees can be seen. It is for the visitors to decide, bearing in mind that a detained person should have a continuous period of 8 hours for rest. This and similar information should be conveyed to the visitors by the escorting officer.

Juveniles

11 Juveniles can be visited in the absence of parental consent provided the juvenile agrees. The custody record can be examined after such a visit, again if the juvenile consents.

12 Where a juvenile is kept in a cell, visitors may ask for an explanation and check the custody record for verification.

General

13 Where a detainee is incapable of giving consent to examine the custody record, the escorting officer should allow access if requested by the visitors.

14 An interview should not be interrupted but visitors may wait until it has ended.

15 You may wish to bring the possibility of a visit to an investigating officer's attention in sensitive cases, given that access can be denied if a superintendent or above judges that

an important case could be prejudiced. Reasons should be entered in the custody record.

16 Conversations between detainees and visitors should normally take place in sight but out of hearing of the escorting officer. If the officer is to remain within hearing, that is a decision for the duty officer or some other senior officer at the station.

Visitors are told that the officer's presence may deter assaults from a violent prisoner.

17 Visitors will show a special interest in detainees who are injured, ill or have some disability.

They may visit detainees in hospital, whether in police custody or not, but will need the hospital authorities' approval.

18 Complaints from the detainee can be about his general treatment or of misconduct by a police officer.

The former should be taken up with the custody officer and the latter reported to the duty officer.

19 A visit report form should be completed and among other things deal with the confidentiality of the visit.

20 The lay visitors will complete a report after each visit. A copy should go to the officer in charge so that any matters needing attention can be dealt with.

During a recent visit some blood was found in a cell and was briefly mentioned in the report. This resulted in a custody officer looking through numerous custody records from another shift to discover the reason behind the blood. This illustrates points made earlier of leaving the custody suite as you would like to find it and checking the suite at the commencement of a tour of duty.

NOTE
A lay visitor CANNOT act as an 'appropriate adult' while acting in the capacity of a 'lay visitor'. (Code C Note 1F and Code D Note 1 D).

BREACH OF THE PEACE, BREACH OF BAIL CONDITIONS

Only where a person is arrested for an offence does Part IV of the PACE Act apply.

However the Codes of Practice apply to any person in custody whether or not they have been arrested for an offence. In relation to breach of bail conditions, courts generally take the view that the person should be detained and produced before them. There are however exceptions, such as juveniles or persons who are ill.

PACE
S 34

C
CODE
1.10

The above, therefore, exempts such persons from the criteria for detention before or after charge and the need for reviews of detention.

NOTE ONE
All persons in custody must be dealt with expeditiously, and released as soon as the need for detention has ceased. However the custody officer will not breach the codes if any delay can be justified, eg, large number of arrests at a football ground may not be granted bail under the provisions of the PACE Act. The custody officer can:

C
CODE
1.1

i) Detain until he can produce before a court, or

ii) Release him unconditionally and ask him to attend court to answer the complaint concerning the breach.

NOTE TWO
If the person fails to appear, the court may summon him to attend. If there is a re-occurrence, or likelihood of a re-occurrence he may be rearrested under common law powers.

DRUG SEARCHES

In the absence of any case law to the contrary the following advice is offered for stop and searches carried out under the drugs legislation.

Persons subject to a stop and search under the drugs legislation in the street, may be removed to the nearest police station in order to carry out the search. Note that it must be the police station nearest to where the suspect was stopped.

Such persons are not arrested but 'detained' under the drugs legislation. A custody record is not required.

A strip search at a police station is allowed under the drugs legislation, but where an intimate search or an intimate sample is necessary then the suspect should be arrested and a superintendent's authority for the search or sample obtained under PACE Act. (See below).

When the suspect is arrested for any offence then the search procedures should be undertaken under the provisions of the PACE Act.

DOMESTIC VIOLENCE

Recently the role of the police has changed. It had been a long standing practice for the police to refer the parties to domestic damage and assaults to their solicitor. This was mainly because, having detained the husband on perhaps a damage offence and taken a statement from the wife, it was quite common for the wife to later retract the statement or say it was his or jointly owned property. Now the police are advised to take an active role in domestic disputes. The custody officer should consider his actions in relation to force policy.

The Domestic Violence and Matrimonial Proceedings Act 1976 provides for a party to a marriage (which includes persons living together as man and wife although not married) to obtain an injunction restraining the other partner from using violence against him or her, or against their children, by excluding the partner from the matrimonial home.

A power of arrest may be attached to an injunction restraining a party to a marriage (or a co-habitee) from using violence against the other party, or a child living with the other party, or from entering the matrimonial home, or a specified area in which the home is included.

NOTE

The procedure for dealing with incidents of domestic violence has changed in relation to charging and custody officers should acquaint themselves with the guidance and directions given by the CPS and their own force instructions, eg the use of section 39 Assault (Criminal Justice Act 1988) in preference to section.47 assault occasioning actual bodily harm AOABH. Section 39, a purely summary offence, replaces section 42 OAPA 1861 (common assault) which has been repealed. In consequence it is now improper to advise complainants in domestic violence cases to pursue their own prosecution under section 42.

Custody officers can authorise the charging (or summons) under section 39 of person arrested under other powers, such as, breach of the peace or section 47 AOABH. In exceptional circumstances, or where the maximum prison sentence under section 39 (6 months) would be inadequate, then a section 47 charge could be used (bearing in mind the accused could elect trial under section 47)

Also of note for custody officers is the fact that section 39 is a 'Recordable Offence' and as such allows, fingerprints, photographs, and intimate and non-intimate samples to be taken.

Police powers

Where a person is in breach of the injunction a police officer may arrest him. Anyone who has been arrested must be bought before a judge within 24 hours (taking no account of Christmas Day, Good Friday, or a Sunday).

A judge should place a time limit on injunctions of no more than three months. Where the danger is thought to still exist towards the end of the three months an application for an extension should be made.

Release after injunction arrest

Q Having arrested and detained a person, can he be released from custody?
A Only where he can't be brought before a court within 24 hours of the arrest. When arrested on an injunction the police cannot release under the 24 hours except on the direction of a judge.

NOTE ONE
In reckoning the 24 hours, no account should be taken of Christmas Day, Good Friday, or any Sunday.

NOTE TWO
The aggrieved party should be informed where a breach of an injunction takes place. This will enable him or her to pursue the breach.

The police should confer with the court officer as to who is responsible for notifying the aggrieved person. In most cases the police would undertake this duty, where practicable, consistent with their other duties.

NOTE THREE
Once the police have placed the person before the court their duty ends. It is for the aggrieved person to present a case to court.

It may not be possible to deliver an offender to prison straight after a court appearance. In these cases, the police may be called upon to keep the person in custody until he can be taken to prison (eg at weekends or public holiday periods).

INDEX